FRIEND W9-DAG-886
OF ACPL

Ben Franklin — Scientist

Other Books by the Same Author

YOUNG PEOPLE'S BOOK OF JET PROPULSION
GUIDED MISSILES

BEN FRANKLIN—
SCIENTIST

by FRANK ROSS, Jr.

ILLUSTRATED WITH LINE DRAWINGS

by AVA MORGAN

J B
F 854 r

LOTHROP, LEE & SHEPARD CO., INC.
NEW YORK

COPYRIGHT, 1952, BY FRANK ROSS, JR.

ALL RIGHTS RESERVED

PRINTED IN THE UNITED STATES OF AMERICA

Contents

U. S. 805469

Ben Franklin — Scientist

CHAPTER ONE

Introduction to Experiment

❖❖❖

IN 1706 THERE lived in Boston the family of Josiah
Franklin, a soap and candle manufacturer. As the new
year arrived, his wife, Abiah, was awaiting the birth
of a child. If the father thought at all about the coming baby, he may have wondered how he would manage to feed another child, for he already had ten boys
and girls.

On the cold winter day of January 17, Abiah Franklin had her son. They named him Benjamin after
Josiah's older brother, his favorite one, who lived with
them. And Benjamin turned out to be their last boy,
though followed by two girls, the final additions to the
family.

The Franklins were poor people. In the fifty-five
years of his parents' marriage, as Benjamin Franklin
later inscribed on the marble stone over their grave,
they owned no wealth nor estate, but "by constant

1

labour and industry, with God's blessing, they maintained a large family comfortably." When the father noticed what a keen mind little Benjamin had, eager and quick to learn, he dreamed of making him a clergyman. But by the time the boy had completed one year at a Boston grammar school, his father sadly realized he could not afford to continue his education. He would have to stay at home and learn the soap and tallow business.

Little did his elders expect, then, that Benjamin would rise above his humble surroundings to do anything outstanding. There was no reason to feel that his life would be any different from that of his forebears— making an honest living by hard work and raising a fine family. But by the end of his life, at the age of eighty-four, this amazing man had played a part in the history of the world that would do credit to any six people combined. First of all, of course, we think of him as Franklin the statesman, who helped write our Declaration of Independence and establish the government of the United States of America. Then we think of him as Franklin the printer and Franklin the writer and philosopher. How, we may well wonder, could one man do all this?

But that was not all. There was also Franklin the scientist and inventor. Everyone learns in school of his famous experiment with the kite in the thunderstorm, but few people study his other experiments with electricity, through which he helped us reach our present-day understanding of this remarkable natural force. You may have heard of the Franklin stove, but you very likely do not know how much work he did to solve the heating problems of colonial America, or some of the funny experiences he had in the course of his experiments. Then there are his dozens of inventions, which he called "contrivances," in every field of life from medicine to music to household equipment.

Often Franklin wished that he could retire from all other work and devote himself completely to science. Had he ever done so, we cannot even guess what mysteries he might have solved, what wonderful inventions he might have produced. But we know that they, too, like those we shall describe here, would have sprung from his brilliance of mind and tremendous physical energy, from his desire to serve his fellowmen, and from his lifelong curiosity about the world of nature.

When the elder Franklin took Benjamin out of school and made him an apprentice in the soap business, the boy very soon became discontented. He did not like his father's trade, which seemed dull and uninteresting. He wanted to go to sea, as his older brother Josiah had done. Living in Boston, where he could run down to the docks, watch the boats come in, and talk with the sailors, how could he not feel the strong pull of the sea? No wonder he rebelled at having to cut wick and run errands.

His father, patiently but firmly, talked him out of

the idea. A life ashore, he said, held many activities worthy of a bright, adventurous young man. Finally young Ben had to promise he would not run off to sea.

After two years of soap-making, however, the father saw that Ben would never make good at that trade. Only for books did he show any great love, reading and studying even on his lunch hour. In his father's little library he found such books as *Pilgrim's Progress, Plutarch's Lives,* De Foe's *Essay on Projects.* Then there was a volume called *Essays to Do Good,* by Dr. Cotton Mather, which perhaps most shaped Franklin's thinking. When, a few years later, he secretly sent some essays in to his brother's paper, he used the name of "Mrs. Silence Dogood." And not long before his death he wrote to Samuel Mather, the son of Cotton Mather, telling him how much these essays had meant to him: "If I have been, as you seem to think, a useful citizen, the public owes the advantage of it to that book."

Well, thought the elder Franklin, Ben might make a good printer, and he apprenticed him to an older son, James. Here Franklin learned thoroughly the pleasant and profitable trade he followed as a grown man. At the same time he could read more books than ever before, also making his first attempts in the field of writing.

Meanwhile, through his love of swimming and boating, Franklin began his career as an inventor. Swimming one day in a neighborhood pond, he asked himself how he could increase his speed in the water. After trying several ideas and giving them up, he hit on what seemed a good plan. If he had larger hands, perhaps he could swim faster.

HAND PADDLE

Shaping two pieces of wood into something like the oval palettes artists use, about ten inches long and six inches wide, he drove a hole through one end of each. Pushing his thumbs through these holes, he held tightly to the palettes and struck out with his natural swimming stroke. Now his hand area was about three times its usual size. Just as he had thought, his speed increased. However, his wrists tired very quickly. That would not do.

Using the same idea, Franklin then carved sandal-like attachments for his feet. But these did not work nearly so well for speed as the hand paddles. Soon Franklin understood why. In swimming, he kicked not only with the soles of his feet, but with their inner parts and ankles as well. Therefore, the sandals acted like anchors and slowed him down.

Although Franklin may have forgotten these extra swimming feet as a boyhood game, the idea proved useful more than two hundred years later. During World War II, the American and British navies employed divers who used an enlarged foot device for undersea work, such as the inspection of the hulls of damaged ships, and for rescue operations. Because of the odd appearance of these artificial feet, the specially trained men who wore them were called "frogmen." Unlike Franklin, they found their foot attachments very helpful in speeding up their work.

One day Franklin was flying his kite on the shore of a large pond near his home. Sitting on the grassy bank, he watched his kite swing to and fro in the blue summer sky. But the rippling water of the pond tempted him more and more. At last, unable to resist any longer, he fastened his kite to a stake in the ground, shed his clothes, and dived into the water.

As he floated happily across the pond, he kept looking toward the kite dancing high overhead in the breeze. Suddenly he thought of something. Why not swim and fly his kite at the same time! Eagerly he climbed out on shore, unloosened the kite string, and dived splashing back into the water. Lying flat on his back again and holding the kite string firmly in his hands, Franklin was slowly pulled along the surface of the pond. When he glanced toward the shore, he saw a friend of his watching in amazement. Calling out to

KITE PULLING FRANKLIN ACROSS THE POND

him, Franklin asked if the friend would carry his little bundle of clothes to a spot across the pond, where he expected to land. Although the pond was almost a mile wide, the young experimenter succeeded in covering the whole distance—getting out on the other side to dress.

Many years later, writing of this incident to a French friend, Franklin wondered whether this method might be used to cross the English Channel, from Dover to Calais. With his usual sense of humor, he concluded that he himself would always prefer to make the trip by packet boat.

After several years in his brother's printing shop, Franklin decided that he could not continue working there. He and James had different ideas about many things. Both stubborn, they often quarreled. Now that he had learned a trade, the younger boy felt sure enough of himself to go on his own. And so, when he was only seventeen, he ran away from home.

He reached Philadelphia alone, almost penniless, with nothing to offer but his knowledge of printing and his determination to succeed. When a printer by the name of Samuel Keimer gave him a job, he decided to make Philadelphia his home. From that time on his years in the city were crowded with the duties of earning a living, marriage, raising a family, political activity, writing, study, and travel.

Somehow he found time, however, to take up again his boyhood hobby of scientific experiments. In 1726, when he was just twenty years old, he was returning on board ship from a two-year visit to England. He had been sent there by Governor Keith of Pennsylvania, who, attracted by Franklin's personality and intelligence, had promised to set the young man up in a printing business of his own. In England he was to buy the necessary equipment for the venture. But when he arrived in London, he received a rude shock. The governor had decided not to go through with the plan, and Franklin was stranded abroad without his return passage. But he did not waste time worrying about it. Instead he promptly set about looking for work in a printing shop and started saving up money to go home.

In Franklin's day it took nearly three months to cross the Atlantic, depending on the wind and the weather. Even for Franklin, who loved the sea, the voyage must have grown tiresome. To pass the time, he kept a diary of his daily experiences aboard the *Berkshire*. He told of visits to different ports before the ship reached the open sea, and described how he and his fellow-passengers spent the long hours aboard. They talked; they played cards and other games; and they observed the world of nature. And during this particular trip nature obliged Franklin the scientist with an eclipse of the sun and an eclipse of the moon.

The first took place on September 14. In his journal Franklin wrote: "This afternoon, about two o'clock it being fair weather and almost calm, as we sat playing draughts upon deck we were surprised with a sudden and unusual darkness of the sun, which as we could perceive, was only covered with a small, thin cloud; when that was passed by we discovered that that glorious luminary laboured under a very great eclipse."

The second event occurred on the last night of September, two weeks from port. Franklin stayed up until almost two o'clock in the morning to watch the cloud over the moon. Again he described the details of the eclipse in his shipboard journal.

Of course, the sea itself offered many curiosities to study. Franklin's notes tell about the different kinds of fish he saw flitting in and out among the waves as well as those the passengers sometimes caught for dinner. Although these descriptions show Franklin's keen eye and wide variety of interests, they do not contain any new discoveries.

As the ship passed through the Gulf Stream, however, Franklin had an opportunity to perform an interesting experiment with a certain kind of crab. In the water of the stream he observed large amounts of gulf weed. Not satisfied with peering at it over the side of the ship, he hauled several samples aboard. While going through a soggy mass of the weed, he noticed one branch which looked different from the rest. On this branch lay something which, though seemingly a part of the weed, resembled a tiny marine animal, "a small shell-fish like a heart, the stalk by which it proceeded from the branch being partly of a grisly kind." A single branch of the weed held about forty of these creatures, "the smallest of them, near the end, containing a substance somewhat like an oyster, but the larger were visibly animated, opening their shells every moment, and thrusting out a set of unformed claws, not unlike those of a crab; but the inner part was still a kind of soft jelly."

Examining his specimen more closely, Franklin spotted a single tiny crab crawling among the clump, yellowish in color like the weed itself. This crab, he believed, had started life as one of those tiny "vegetable animals" crawling about it. If so, the rest of his "odd kind of fruit" would probably turn into crabs also. Why not, if caterpillars could turn into butterflies?

To test his theory, Franklin placed the sample of seaweed in salt water and waited to see what would happen. The next day he found another baby crab on the weed. More sure than ever of the truth of his theory about the reproduction of this kind of crab, Franklin, much to his disappointment, could not complete the experiment. In spite of the salt water, the seaweed quickly withered, and the tiny embryonic crabs died.

None of these notes and experiments, of course, gained major importance in Franklin's career. Nevertheless, they did show his deep curiosity about the world of nature and his knack for thinking up simple yet sound experiments to test his theories. In later years the marine world again served as Franklin's laboratory for a number of more valuable discoveries. But meanwhile he turned his attention more profitably to problems on land.

When he was about twenty-three or twenty-four years old, he performed what appears to be his first major experiment: a number of tests to see whether the heat of the sun would affect cloth of different colors in different ways. Probably he first reported his findings to a club he had organized, called the Junto, a group of friends all interested in scientific and technical subjects. Every Friday evening they met at a nearby tavern or at each other's homes to talk about science, philosophy, and books. Often they read aloud their own papers describing their various experiments.

However, Franklin lost his original notes on this early study of his. When he was fifty-five years old, he retold the story from memory in a letter to young Mary Stevenson of London: "I took a number of little square pieces of broadcloth from a tailor's pattern card of various colours. There were black, deep blue, lighter blue, green, purple, red, yellow, white and other colours or shades of colours. I laid them all out upon the snow in a bright sunshiny morning. In a few hours (I cannot now be exact as to the time) the black, being warmed most by the sun, was sunk so low as to be below the stroke of the sun's rays; the dark blue almost as low, the lighter blue not quite so much as the dark, the other colours less as they were lighter; and the white remained on the surface of the snow, not having entered it at all."

Here Franklin suggested an easy test that Mary could make herself. On the first sunny day that came along, she could take a little walk in her garden, wearing a dress made partly of white cloth and partly of black. After fifteen minutes, if she touched the cloth of her dress, she would find the white part still pretty cool and the black part very warm against her hand.

Another experiment Franklin outlined for Mary called for the use of a magnifying glass and a sheet of paper, part of it clear white and part covered with dark spots. If she held the glass so that the sun was focused on each part of the paper in turn and timed it while it burned, she would find that the spotted section burned faster than the white.

Whenever Franklin made a discovery, he wanted to find a way to put it to practical use. In his letter he listed the ways in which this knowledge about heat and colors could help mankind. If people in hot, sunny climates would wear light-colored or white clothes, they could enjoy much greater comfort, since these would not absorb the heat of the sun as much as darker clothes. This would prove valuable to people living in the tropics, to people everywhere in the summer season, and to soldiers and sailors, who often did hard physical work which made them become greatly overheated. By wearing white summer hats, both men and women could avoid possible sickness caused by the direct rays of the sun.

Aside from its use in the selection of clothes, Franklin saw how his new discovery could improve agriculture. If a fruit tree grew near a stone wall, the owner should paint the wall black. Then it would absorb the heat of the sun during the day and remain warm long after nightfall, thus giving the tree some protection against frost. At the same time the heat sent forth by the painted wall would make the tree grow more rapidly.

Only in very recent years has the study of color and its effects on people attracted much attention. Today it has reached the stage of scientific investigation. Franklin's understanding of its importance two centuries ago shows his remarkable approach to science with an insight far ahead of his time.

Almost ten years passed before Franklin made his next major contribution to science and invention. During that time he did not lose interest in this field, however, often printing in his newspaper, the *Pennsylvania Gazette,* articles on some natural wonder, such as earthquakes and storms, or some mechanical problem. No doubt he continued making experiments in private. But for the most part he devoted his energies to earning a living and to an increasing interest in political affairs.

Then, in 1740, at the age of thirty-four, Franklin entered a new phase of his career, bringing forth his first great invention, the Pennsylvania fireplace.

CHAPTER TWO

Heating in Colonial America

❖❖

IN FRANKLIN'S DAY most families still used the open hearth or fireplace not only as a cooking stove but also to heat their homes. Because of the old-fashioned construction of their fireplaces, however, the colonists suffered much discomfort. Sitting close to the fire they would be too warm, but only a few feet away they would be cold. Also, much of the smoke, instead of disappearing through the chimney, drifted into the room, poisoning the air and blackening the walls and furniture.

Discouraged by these factors, people imported stoves from Holland and Germany, which they hoped would be an improvement, at least somewhat, over the fireplace. They even tried a type of heating equipment which consisted of a charcoal-burning iron pot hung from a metal tripod placed in the center of the room.

But none of these new methods brought much improvement.

Like all his fellow-colonists, Franklin wanted to solve this annoying household problem. Unlike most of the others, however, he soon began experimenting to discover both cause and remedy. The first sign of his interest appeared when he presented to the Junto the question, "How Can Smokey Chimneys Be Cured?" Perhaps Franklin himself could not foresee how many long years of thought and research it would take before he could provide a good answer, though even then not what he considered a complete one. Not until 1785 did he write his long letter on the subject to Dr. Jan Ingenhousz which was later published as a pamphlet called *The Cause and Cure of Smokey Chimneys*.

But as yet the young inventor had only many questions and a few unproved theories. To determine the characteristics of air, both cold and heated, he performed several simple experiments. In the first he placed an ordinary glass bottle near a fire. As the air in the bottle became warm and expanded, Franklin noticed that some of it escaped through the opening. Then he turned the bottle upside down, placing its neck in a pan of water. As the air in the bottle grew cool, the water rose through the neck, until it filled the space previously taken by the air that had been forced out. Now Franklin held a piece of hot coal near the bottle, once more raising the temperature of the air inside it. Again the air expanded, this time forcing the water out of the bottle.

From this test it appeared that air is a great deal lighter once it has been rarefied and expanded by heat, therefore rising when it comes in contact with normal or cool air. But Franklin needed further proof to satisfy him of the truth of his theory. In his second experiment he relied again on the simplest tools, using a rubber bladder, perhaps a little like those used in basketballs and soccer balls. After partly filling the bladder with air, he placed it near a blazing hearth. In a few minutes the heat of the fire started to warm the air in the bladder, which soon expanded to its full capacity. Then Franklin removed it from the fire and placed it in a cool spot, upon which the air cooled off and contracted until the bladder shrank down to its original shape.

These observations helped Franklin to understand the failings of the open hearth, particularly in throwing the smoke back into a room. They helped him, furthermore, to plan a stove of his own design, a stove which would make the colonial home a more comfortable and attractive place to live in.

From the time of its appearance in 1740, Franklin's Pennsylvania fireplace, later nicknamed the Franklin stove, proved a great success. Made of cast iron, it was designed to be taken apart and moved easily from room to room. Since it was intended for use with the

THE FRANKLIN STOVE

ordinary fireplace, the stove generally stood on the brick flooring in front of the hearth, which required only two changes for this purpose.

Under the stove several of the bricks had to be removed to form an air passage leading to the air box, a unit inside the stove. Directly behind the stove, about four inches from the wall of the chimney proper, a false back or partition was put up, extending a considerable distance above the stove. From the top of this false back a shutter reached across to the inner side of the mantelpiece. The false back served as a barrier to guide the rising smoke into the chimney proper. With the shutter closing off the opening into the room, the smoke could not drift back in.

Shortly after introducing his new stove, Franklin turned over its manufacture and sale to Robert Grace, a friend of his who operated an iron products factory.

DIAGRAM OF THE FRANKLIN
STOVE'S OPERATION

19

To encourage sales, the inventor wrote an advertising pamphlet describing the various features of his stove. According to his autobiography, he called the booklet "An Account of the Newly Invented Pennsylvania Fireplaces; wherein their Construction and Manner of Operation is particularly explained; their Advantages above every other Method of warming Rooms demonstrated; and all Objections that have been raised against the Use of them answered and obviated."

Of the fourteen advantages Franklin claimed for his stove, he naturally described first its heating powers: "1. That your whole room is equally warmed; so that people need not crowd so close round the fire, but may sit near the window, and have the benefit of the light for reading, writing, needle-work, etc. . . . 2. If you sit near the fire, you have not that cold draught of uncomfortable air nipping your back and heels, as when before common fires, by which many catch cold, being scorcht before, and, as it were, froze behind."

Among other things, one of the most important was its economy in burning fuel. When he installed a working model in his own room, said Franklin, it gave far more heat with only one-fourth the amount of fuel consumed by other types of heating equipment. To housewives he pointed out that the new stove cured "most smokey chimneys, and thereby preserves both the eyes and the furniture." Finally, the stove was attractive in appearance and useful for miscellaneous purposes such as boiling water for tea, warming flatirons, or keeping food hot."

Despite the superiority of the Franklin stove, a number of objections had already arisen. Some people complained that at times the stove produced too much heat, making the family more susceptible to colds. Others spread the rumor that the cast iron gave off an unpleasant and unhealthy odor.

With complete frankness the inventor told his critics that if they had any complaint, they must find fault with their own habits and not with the construction of the stove. Often in those days people would test the temperature of a stove by spitting on it. Naturally, Franklin pointed out, continual spitting on a hot stove would leave a foul smell. Sometimes, too, people carelessly placed candles on the fireplace. When the heat melted the wax, the soft liquid ran over on the stove itself, producing an odor of scorched wax. With very little care, Franklin insisted, the new stove could be kept clean and objectionable smells avoided.

Soon Governor Thomas of Pennsylvania, having read the pamphlet describing the stove, became an enthusiastic supporter of the new invention, offering Franklin a patent which would guarantee him the sole rights for some years to its manufacture and sale. Although most people would have been glad of this privilege, Franklin refused to accept it. Already he had dedicated himself to the unselfish betterment of his world, a world in which most of the physical comforts we enjoy today were not only unknown but undreamed of. From his contributions to science and technology he wanted no personal profit, declaring, "As we enjoy great advantages from the inventions of others, we should be glad of an opportunity to serve others by any invention of ours; and this we should do freely and generously."

Unfortunately, Franklin's unselfish philosophy did not inspire many people to follow his example. When an iron-monger in London read Franklin's pamphlet, he decided to capitalize on the American's invention by building a similar stove and taking out a patent on it in England. Of course, he made a few minor changes in the design, but he used most of the features introduced by Franklin. Later it turned out that the English stove, though altered only slightly, was not as good as Franklin's. By that time, however, the iron-monger had sold a large number of stoves and made a great deal of money.

Nevertheless, Franklin did not regret his decision not to patent his invention, and he took no legal action against the Englishman. In his autobiography he wrote: "This is not the only instance of patents taken out for my inventions by others, tho' not always with the same success, which I never contested, as having no desire of profiting by patents myself, and hating disputes."

With the Pennsylvania fireplace an established success, many an inventor in Franklin's place would have rested on his laurels and stopped thinking about stoves and chimneys. Not so this colonial master-of-all-trades. Throughout the many years of his long and productive life, stoves and their operation held a particular fascination for his inventive talents.

Many years later in London, at the age of sixty-five, Franklin actually designed a second stove. This he called the "smoke consuming stove," basing its construction on an idea introduced by a French scientist, who had found a way to burn fuel in an extremely efficient manner and with very little smoke. At a demonstration of the method, Franklin was keenly impressed. He quickly grasped the basic workings of this heating device. "Its principle is that of a siphon reversed, operating on air in a manner somewhat similar to the operation of the common siphon on water." But Franklin saw, too, how it could be vastly improved, especially in appearance.

The design for his own "smoke consuming stove" took shape in Franklin's mind shortly afterward. Built on the lines of a large vase, its shape made it not only more attractive, but also ideally suited for burning coal, the type of fuel for which this stove was intended. For those people who lived in areas where coal was scarce or unattainable, Franklin worked out an alternate design for a wood-burning model. Shaped like a square chest, it had the same operating characteristics as the coalstove and the same "smoke consuming" feature.

In the space where a fire would ordinarily be set in a hearth, Franklin cemented an ironplate to the floor. The plate was honeycombed with six metal partitions set at right angles to the bottom, three fastened to the back plate of the stove and three to the front. They did not extend completely across but stopped several inches from the front and back sides. The result was a twisting passageway, not unlike the mazes children are fond of playing with that, in order to reach the center, require them to follow with a pencil a series of swirling lines broken at intervals.

These partitions arose about four inches from the bottom plate. Directly on top of this arrangement Franklin placed another metal cover with a small square-shaped opening in the center which contained parallel bars of metal. Narrow metal plates were then fastened onto the four sides of this boxlike structure, enclosing it completely. The two front metal panels were movable to permit the cleaning out of the ashes.

On top of this closed-in base Franklin installed still another box, a great deal smaller than the bottom one, which fitted directly over the small grate. This, too, had a movable plate in front so that one could clean out residue that formed in the chamber after a fire. In the center of the top plate was a small hole through which the smoke could pass from the upper to the lower chamber.

Directly over this hole Franklin placed a rather large metal urn. This was the fire chamber proper, held firmly in position by two fixed pins rising from the smaller box. At the very tip of the urn was an ornamental brass knob designed as a flame. Through a small opening at the top of this hollow knob air flowed to help stimulate the fire.

Usually the "smoke consuming stove" was set up in a sealed-off fireplace or in a special niche near the chimney, connected to the flue by two small pipes. Since the fire did not really consume all the smoke, some means had to be provided for the remaining smoke to escape. For this purpose two small openings were cut in the bottom directly back of the rear plate of the stove.

Writing about his second stove to a French friend, Marquis de Turgot, Franklin said, "The funnel of the chimney (to which the stove is connected) is the longer leg, the vase the shorter; and as in the common siphon the weight of water in the longer leg is greater than that in the shorter leg, and thus in descending permits the water in the shorter leg to rise by the pressure of the atmosphere; so in this aerial siphon the levity of the air in the longer leg being greater than that in the shorter, it rises and permits the pressure of the atmosphere to force that in the shorter to descend. This causes the smoke to descend also, and in passing through burning coals it is kindled into flame, thereby heating more the passages in the iron box whereon the vase which contains the coals is placed, and retarding at the same time the consumption of the coals."

Franklin was extremely pleased with his second stove, which heated a room very well. After using it for three winters in London and one year in France, he finally brought it back to his own home in Philadelphia. As with his Pennsylvania fireplace, Franklin quickly pointed out the good features of his "smoke consuming stove." The main advantage, the consumption of smoke, in turn helped keep chimneys free of soot and produced good heat with a minimum of fuel. And as Franklin further wrote in his letter to Marquis de Turgot: "It is capable of being used to advantage in our kitchens, if one could overcome the repugnance of cooks to the using of new instruments and new methods."

During his years of research on heating problems, Franklin often came upon facts which perhaps had no bearing on the immediate project at hand. These bits of information and ideas he carefully stored away in his mind for future reference, often using them later to good advantage. In this way, through his study of chimney functions, he eventually developed his sliding plate invention.

At that time, about 1758, he was also in London as political agent for the Colony of Pennsylvania. His hostess there was Mary Stevenson's mother, whose home on Craven Street in London frequently served as Franklin's English headquarters. To perfect his sliding plate, or draft attachment, Franklin worked at Mrs. Stevenson's fireplace. First he made the front opening of the hearth smaller, until it measured about two feet by three feet. Underneath the top of the fireplace, where the opening of the chimney made its entrance into the

26

hearth proper, Franklin then fastened into place an iron frame which extended to the back wall of the chimney. In this frame he cut grooves, into which he inserted a metal plate of nearly the same size as the frame. By regulating this movable piece of metal, the opening of the chimney could be cut off completely or adjusted to any size, serving a purpose similar to that of the present-day damper.

Said Franklin in a letter: "This plate is just so large as to fill the whole space, and shut the chimney entirely when thrust quite in, which is convenient when there is no fire. Drawing it out, so as to leave a space between its further edge and the back, of about two inches; this space is sufficient for the smoke to pass, and so large a part of the funnel being stopped by the rest of the plate, the passage of warm air out of the room, up the chimney, is obstructed and retarded, and by that means much cold air is prevented from coming in through crevices to supply its place."

Not only did this sliding draft help the fireplace throw more heat back into the room, but it also helped to save fuel. Several of Franklin's London friends, after attending a demonstration of his invention, had the device installed in their own hearths and found that it lived up to all his promises.

In the course of his work on stoves and on the sliding draft, Franklin learned a good many facts about fireplaces and chimneys. Among other things, he had noticed that during the summer months a draft of air flowed constantly through the fireplace and up the chimney. Noting the cool, dry quality of the draft, his alert mind saw an excellent opportunity to convert the fireplace into a practical cold-storage closet during the fireless months of the year.

At once he proceeded to build one in his Philadelphia home. Making a light wooden frame, he fitted it snugly into the opening of the hearth. To this frame he tacked a piece of cloth porous enough to allow the air to flow through. The main function of the cloth was to protect from flies the food stored inside. In addition, it concealed the unattractive appearance of the frame.

Then Franklin built another wooden frame, which he put into position within the fireplace itself. This he equipped with hooks on which to hang various food articles, especially meat. Before he put the food in the box, he wrapped it in clean cloths to protect it from the dust that naturally filled the fireplace. With meat, the cloths had to be kept constantly moist. The dripping water fell into a shallow tray underneath. Cooled by the continuous passage of air, meat remained fresh for a week or more in the hottest weather, dairy products also keeping for some time.

Certainly Franklin never expected, while studying heating equipment, to invent a cold storage box. But with his keen perception, he eagerly seized and developed each new idea. In his day the problem of food spoilage begged attention, and though we may consider his fireplace refrigerator extremely crude, it nevertheless contributed a good deal toward easing the situation, making colonial life just a little bit more comfortable.

Gradually Franklin accumulated more and more knowledge about stoves and chimneys, but his many activities long kept him from getting his thoughts on the subject down on paper. Finally, when he was almost eighty, the opportunity came. After long years of service in Europe for the American colonies, he was again sailing for home. To fill the tedious hours of this voyage, his eighth and last across the Atlantic, he took up his pen to set down the record of his lifelong scientific research.

Although the story was long enough for a small book, Franklin sent it as his reply to a letter from his good friend, Dr. Jan Ingenhousz, who had written asking him for information concerning the defects of chimneys in use at that time. As we have said, the letter later appeared as a pamphlet for the general public, called *The Cause and Cure of Smokey Chimneys.*

Here Franklin explained why chimneys often threw smoke back into a room. Then he listed specific methods he had developed for getting chimneys to work properly. In his letter he described several of his experiments on the nature of smoke and his suggestions for improved construction of chimneys and fireplaces.

Franklin observed, however, that no matter how well informed a man might be on a particular subject, he would still meet problems that would tax his skill, and sometimes even baffle him completely. Once in London a friend asked him for help. Of a number of chimneys on his house, one presented a problem. Every time the family built a fire in this particular hearth, the smoke billowed right back into the room.

Franklin, of course, agreed to investigate the trouble. First he built a fire in the defective fireplace. The smoke indeed poured out of the fireplace opening and into the room. Thinking that perhaps the fire lacked sufficient air, he opened the door of the room. But the chimney still smoked. Perhaps the fireplace opening was too large. Franklin erected a temporary partition around it to make it smaller. Alas, the smoke continued to float into the room instead of up the chimney.

Franklin went outdoors and carefully examined the chimney, but not, as things turned out, carefully enough. Finally he had to leave without finding the cause of the trouble. Some months later his friend, however, succeeded in finding it himself. After his house had been built, it seems, it remained unoccupied for several years. During that time a family of birds saw in this one chimney a splendid location for a nest. No wonder this chimney later smoked, cluttered as it was with nest-building materials! Once cleaned out, Franklin's friend wrote him, it worked perfectly.

To Franklin this incident proved further that no one man can think of everything. Indeed, although he had plumbed the depths of this subject as no man had before him, he knew that there was room for further research and urged continued study in the field. For better results he suggested using a model, made of glass, including a number of rooms with fireplaces and chimneys, an exact replica of a real home. Candles could be burned in the tiny fireplaces, creating conditions of a normal hearth in operation. Thus one could observe every detail of the fire and its rising smoke, learning a great deal more, Franklin believed. Today the idea of work models is almost universally accepted in science and engineering.

In encouraging others to follow up on his work, Franklin showed the vision of a true scientist, concerned not with praise for his contributions but with continued enlightenment.

CHAPTER THREE

Musical Glasses

❖❖❖

WHEN WE READ about Franklin and think of his work in science and politics, we can hardly imagine him in a gay, laughing mood. But, like almost every truly great man, he had a deep sense of humor and good fellowship. His fun-loving spirit and great warmth bubbled up now and then even in the wisdom of "Poor Richard." Once, for example, he proposed an hourglass which would disrupt the neighborhood by shooting off cannonlike chimes. In the pages of his *Almanac*, too, he printed many of his delightful fables for "good children."

Often, after his day's work was done, Franklin loved to spend an evening with his friends, joking and singing. In music Franklin enjoyed his greatest relaxation, and many of the melodies he and his friends sang had words composed by Franklin, such as "The Mother

Country" and his "Sailor Song." The most popular, however, was one dedicated to his wife and called "My Plain Country Joan." With his many interests, of course, he wrote songs about various subjects.

Wherever he went, therefore, Franklin naturally took an interest in musical activities. And so, in England in the late 1750's, he heard of a strange musical instrument known as musical glasses. By that time Franklin had won admission, for his electrical discoveries, to the Royal Society of London. There he met an English member of the Society, Edmund Hussey Delaval, who had built a musical glass instrument as an improvement over one designed by another man, Richard Puckeridge of Ireland.

When Delaval announced a demonstration of his instrument, Franklin eagerly attended. Instantly enchanted by its beautiful, sweet tones, he nevertheless considered it poorly designed and too difficult to play. It consisted simply of a number of water glasses of several sizes set up on a table top, each glass filled to a different level with water to give off its particular tone. To play the musical glasses, the musician passed his finger tips over the brims of the glasses.

Quickly Franklin's mechanical instinct went to work. First he designed special glasses, "the largest . . . nine inches in diameter, and the smallest three inches," with twenty-three sizes in between, each varying only a quarter of an inch from the next. Shaped like hemispheres, each had "an open neck or socket in the middle," where the glass was thickest, gradually thinning out toward the edges.

Franklin's most difficult job was tuning the glasses to get the proper tone from each. Finally he succeeded "by grinding them round from the neck towards the brim, the breadth of one or two inches . . . often trying the glass by a well-tuned harpsichord, comparing the tone drawn from the glass by your finger with the note you want, as sounded by that string of the harpsichord." With what patience Franklin worked! "When you come nearer the matter," he wrote, "be careful to wipe the glass clean and dry before each trial, because the tone is something flatter when the glass is wet . . . and grinding a very little between each trial, you will thereby tune to great exactness. The more care is necessary in this because, if you go below your required tone, there is no sharpening it again but by grinding somewhat off the brim, which will afterward require polishing and thus increase the trouble."

When each glass played just the right note, Franklin marked it by name with a diamond. After he had tuned all the glasses, he arranged them in a single unit on an iron rod or spindle tapering down from an inch at its thick end to an eighth of an inch at the other. To attach them to the rod, he inserted into the neck of each one, a cork, which he pierced and fitted securely to the spindle, placing the glasses one inside another from the largest at the thick end of the spindle down to the smallest at the thin end.

U. S 05469

His imagination still at work, Franklin decided to use color "to distinguish the glasses the more readily to the eye." From Franklin's own word-picture we can see how attractive the instrument must have looked: "My largest glass is G, a little below the reach of a common voice, and my highest G, including three octaves. . . . I have painted the apparent parts of the glasses within side, every semi-tone white, and the other notes of the octave . . . C, red; D, orange; E, yellow; F, green; G, blue; A, indigo; B, purple; and C, red again; so that glasses of the same colour (the white excepted) are always octaves to each other."

Now Franklin set up his instrument in a wooden case "about three feet long, eleven inches every way wide within at the biggest end, and five inches at the smallest end." Thus Franklin designed his case to follow the conelike shape of the instrument itself. "This case," he wrote, "opens in the middle of its height, and the upper part turns up by hinges fixed behind. The spindle, which is of hard iron, lies horizontally from end to end . . . and is made to turn on brass gudgeons at each end." Supported by four legs, the case included two drawers for music sheets and other supplies.

To play the instrument, the musician sat before it as he would at a piano. Now and then he moistened his fingers with a wet sponge, for the slightest bit of grease in his touch could spoil the music. Sometimes he rubbed a little chalk on his finger tips to help him catch better hold of the glass rims and get richer tones.

By a light or heavy pressure of his fingers he could play softly or loudly, depending on the effect he wanted.

As with a piano, too, the player must use not only his hands but his feet. During the performance, the glasses had to turn round and round on their spindle. However, since the musician needed both hands for fingering the rims, Franklin had designed a foot treadle for setting the instrument in motion. From the spindle, wrote Franklin, "a square shank comes . . . through the box, on which shank a wheel is fixed by a screw. This wheel serves as a fly to make the motion equable when the spindle, with the glasses, is turned by the foot like a spinning wheel. My wheel is mahogany, eighteen inches in diameter, and pretty thick. . . . An ivory pin is fixed in the face of this wheel. . . . Over the neck of this pin is put a loop of the string that comes up from the movable step to give it motion."

The direction in which the instrument turned, Franklin pointed out, made a difference in the music. For the finest tone he believed it should move away from the finger tips, not toward them.

Franklin had taken the old "musical glasses" a long way from the simple ambitions of Puckeridge and Delaval. How could he content himself with using their ordinary name for the instrument! No, he must find a new one to give it a new place in the world of music. Finally he chose "armonica," the Italian word for *harmonious*. In a letter to an Italian friend, Giambatista Baccaria, describing his instrument as "peculiarly adapted to Italian music, especially that of the soft and plaintive kind," he said he had named it "in honor of your musical language." In later years people called it the harmonica, a name which has been adopted in our own times for a mouth instrument boys often like to play.

At last Franklin introduced his armonica to the musical public. Always a good salesman, he pointed out its special features, among them the fact that, unlike the harpsichord and the piano, it never needed

ARMONICA

re-tuning. But most of all he praised the beauty of its music, lovelier, he believed, than that of the original musical glasses.

Once the manufacture of the armonica got under way in London, its fame quickly spread far and wide. Marianne Davies, an English musician, toured the Continent in 1762 in a series of armonica recitals. Not only in England, but in France and Italy, Germany and Austria, she charmed music lovers with her playing of the new instrument. Kings and queens applauded Miss Davies, and Marie Antoinette took lessons from her.

After this first success, other musicians took up the armonica, conducting regular concerts throughout Europe. Before long some of the great composers of the day, like Mozart and Beethoven, shared the enthusiasm for Franklin's instrument, composing a number of selections intended especially for the armonica.

In colonial America the armonica made its first public appearance in 1764. This performance took place in Philadelphia, at the Assembly Room of Lodge Alley. How proud the whole town must have felt that night—of the brilliant citizen who forty years earlier had come as a runaway boy knocking at its door!

Of course, Franklin always had an armonica at home. All-around man that he was, he not only enjoyed listening to music, but could also play several instruments, among them the harp, the guitar, and the violin. Now, when friends dropped in, he often entertained them by playing a few pieces on his own armonica.

For about fifty years the armonica enjoyed great popularity. Finally, however, it dropped out of use. No one knows exactly why this happened. Perhaps the vibrations of the glasses placed too heavy a strain on the nerves of the musician. Gradually, one after another gave it up, its beautiful tones silenced at last.

But Franklin had won his place in musical history. Today we consider his other work more important. But more than anything else except his electrical discoveries, the whole world of the eighteenth century cheered his contribution to music, not for his composing ability, or for the instruments he played, but for his clever design of an attractive, professional armonica from a clumsy, cumbersome set of musical glasses.

CHAPTER FOUR

Making Life Easier

✧✧

IN THE HISTORY of a period rich with great men, Franklin still shines out to many as the greatest. Carl Van Doren, a noted writer on Franklin's life, has compared him to the tallest in a range of mountains, one that "towers above the others, which are, in a sense, only foothills to it." And perhaps because of his very greatness, Franklin never thought any subject too small for his attention.

A lesser man might have been afraid people would laugh at him for dabbling with what Franklin called his "contrivances." Franklin, however, never passed through any phase of daily life without thinking of a way to make it more pleasant. No doubt he had a lot of fun, too, with this lifelong hobby picked up in boyhood, possibly from watching his father, who, he remembered, "had a mechanical genius too, and, on occasion, was very handy in the use of other trades-men's tools."

Everyone has seen the grocer take down cans and boxes of food from the highest shelves with a pair of prongs attached to a long stick. Maybe you have wondered how he would ever manage without this "long arm." Few people today know that Franklin invented this gadget. Of course he may not have realized how helpful it would be in a grocery. But libraries have shelves, too, and as Franklin grew older, he found it harder and harder to reach the books up at the top.

His first idea was to build a combination chair and ladder. By lifting the seat, lo and behold, you had a small ladder! Nowadays your mother has one a little like it in her kitchen and your father in his workshop.

By the time Franklin was eighty, however, often suffering from gout and dizziness, he could no longer use the ladder. Never stumped, he went to work on his new gadget. To an eight-foot length of pine an inch thick he fastened two thin extensions. In each of these he drilled a small hole, through which he threaded strong cord, knotted at one end to keep it from slipping out. At the other end Franklin made a loop of the cord. Thus the "long arm" was born.

Raising the stick with its extensions turned upward, he placed one hand in the loop and pulled the cord straight down the side of the arm, which he held firmly with the other hand. Then he slid the extensions around the book he wanted. "The laths being flexible,"

LONG ARM

he explained, "you may easily by a slight pressure side-
ways open them wider if the book is thick, or close
them if it is thin by pulling the string, so as to enter the
shorter lath or thumb between your book and that
which is next to its other side, then push till the back
of your book comes to touch the string. Then draw the
string or sinew tight, which will cause the thumb and
finger to pinch the book strongly, so that you may
draw it out."

Although "all new tools require some practice,"
Franklin boasted that "this requires very little."

As the years passed, too, Franklin needed eye-
glasses, not only for reading but for ordinary vision.
What a nuisance to have to change glasses every time
he put down his book or came back from a walk! On
his frequent travels he found this especially awkward,
for he "sometimes read, and often wanted to regard the
prospects."

FRANKLIN'S BIFOCALS

Finally he wrote, "I had the glasses cut, and half of each kind associated in the same circle. . . . By this means, as I wear my spectacles constantly, I have only to move my eyes up or down, as I want to see distinctly far or near, the proper glasses being always ready."

Oddly enough, Franklin claimed, his new glasses improved his French! "When one's ears are not well accustomed to the sounds of a language, a sight of the movements in the features of him that speaks helps to explain; so that I understand French better by the help of my spectacles."

During one of his visits to England, in about 1760, while staying at the home of Mrs. Stevenson, Franklin spent some of his leisure time making a rather unusual clock. It had only three wheels and one hand which showed hours, minutes, and seconds. Long after Franklin had forgotten all about his clock, a friend of his, James Ferguson, and another man, John Whitehurst, carried on this work by bringing out slightly altered models.

All these mechanical conveniences, in a way, sprang from Franklin's concern with good citizenship. As a lad of sixteen, in the spring of 1722, he had made "a resolution, to do for the future, all that *lies in my way* for the service of my countrymen." This he pledged in an article which, after signing it with the curious pen name of Mrs. Silence Dogood, he slipped under the door of his brother's printing shop. If up to that time, as he wrote, he had "been very deficient in this particular," he certainly more than made up his share afterward.

In 1736 Franklin organized the first fire department in Philadelphia, known as the Union Fire Company. Later he led the city in starting its first street-cleaning department and suggested improvements in the police department. Besides setting up America's first public library, he helped found the Pennsylvania Hospital and the first college in Pennsylvania, still in existence as the state university.

Although Franklin is often credited with the invention of the street lamp, he actually got this idea from a neighbor of his, John Clifton. Even in that day, dark streets harbored thugs and hoodlums, who all too often disturbed the peace of colonial Philadelphia. When Mr. Clifton erected a street lamp in front of his home, Franklin saw in it an inspiration for a civic improvement. Through his newspapers he urged the city government to provide such lamps for the whole community. Of course, Franklin gave Mr. Clifton proper credit, but people have often thought of the idea as Franklin's.

After the city adopted the plan for street lighting, however, another difficulty developed. Since the lamps were lit with oil, the flame created a good bit of soot. The glass globes imported from England and erected on the lamp posts had no opening through which the smoke could escape. To have them cleaned every day involved both trouble and expense. Often, too, the cleaner would accidentally bump the glass against the post or even drop it, shattering it into a thousand pieces.

Franklin therefore suggested "composing them of four flat panes with a long funnel above to draw up the smoke; the crevices admitting air below, to facilitate the ascent of the smoke; by this means they were kept clean, and did not grow dark in a few hours, as the London lamps do, but continu'd bright till morning,

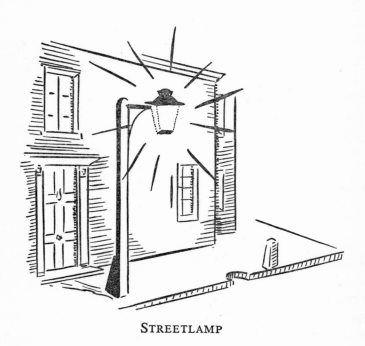

STREETLAMP

and an accidental stroke would generally break but a single pane, easily repaired."

His design of a new lamp, indeed Franklin's own idea, perhaps helped confuse people into calling him the inventor of street lighting.

In civic welfare, public health, of course, plays an important part. Although he sometimes apologized for "meddling" with the medical profession, Franklin could not restrain himself. A seed once planted in the rich soil of his mind, it blossomed like a wild flower in spite of himself.

In 1752, for example, his brother John developed a bladder ailment. European physicians often recommended treatment with an instrument called the flexible catheter, not available, however, in colonial America. That December, Franklin wrote to his brother: "Reflecting yesterday on your desire to have a flexible catheter, a thought struck into my mind, how one might probably be made, and lest you should not readily conceive it by any description of mine, I went immediately to the silversmith's and gave directions for making one (sitting by till it was finished) that it might be ready for this post."

Forty years later he could still come up with an idea for doctors. When his friend Alexander Small wrote him, in 1789, about his trouble with hearing, Franklin replied: "The deafness you complain of gives me concern; if great, it must diminish considerably your pleasure in conversation. If moderate, you may remedy it easily and readily, by putting your thumb and fingers behind your ear, pressing it outwards, and enlarging it, as it were, with the hollow of your hand. By an exact experiment, I found that I could hear the tick of a watch at forty-five feet distance by this means, which was barely audible at twenty feet without it. The experiment was made at midnight when the house was still."

Always ahead of his times, Franklin recognized the danger of contagion in spreading the common cold. In 1773 he jotted down a note for a paper on the subject which he never got around to writing. "Most people," read the note, "think they get cold by coming *out* of such hot rooms; they get them by being *in*."

Unlike many of his fellow-colonists, too, he had no superstitious fears of innoculation against disease. When his four-year-old son Francis died of smallpox, the rumor spread that he had caught it through innoculation. Stricken as he was with personal grief, Franklin knew how much harm this false story could do. Immediately he printed in one of his newspapers an item explaining that the child had picked up the infection "in the usual way." In fact, Franklin had intended to have him innoculated and felt sure that would have saved him. But, since the boy had not yet recovered from a previous illness, Franklin kept putting it off. He never forgave himself for this "neglect" and for the death of his little "Frankie."

Throughout his life Franklin carried on the spirit

which had inspired him at the age of twenty-one to organize his club, the Junto, "the spirit of inquiry after truth, without fondness for dispute, or desire of victory."

CHAPTER FIVE

Electrical Studies and Discoveries

✧✧✧

BENEATH BENJAMIN FRANKLIN'S tremendous inventive energy lay the mainspring of his genius, his thirst for scientific knowledge. Curiosity about the nature of the world grows naturally out of an "inquiry after truth."

From the time he made notes, at the age of twenty, on the eclipse of the moon and the eclipse of the sun, he dreamed of a day when, retired from business, he could devote himself to scientific experiment. Alas for this castle-in-the-air! Destiny forced him to remain a part-time scientist. For although he gained financial security by the age of forty-two, he gave up working for his living only to work for the government, first of the colonies and later of the young United States of America.

In Franklin's day European scientists started a revival of interest in the mysteries of electricity. Although electrical power had been recognized from the earliest days of the Greeks and Romans, no one had yet figured out very much about it. Ancient man had noticed that if he rubbed certain objects or materials together, he stirred up this strange and wonderful element. Later scientists, using the word *friction*, which means *rubbing*, coined the phrase "frictional electricity." This they further broke down into two kinds of frictional electricity: "vitreous," produced by rubbing a glass tube with silk; and "resinous," by rubbing the tube with resin, wool, or fur.

Sometime about the middle of the eighteenth century a Dutch scientist, Pieter van Musschenbroek, made a new discovery in the field of electrical research. Using a jar of the kind in which his wife might have preserved fruits and jellies, he covered it with tin foil about three-quarters of the way up, inside and out. Through the neck of the bottle ran a length of wire attached on the inside to the tin foil and on the outside to a small metal knob. The wire transmitted electricity from the jar for use in experiments.

The Leyden Jar, named after the city in Holland where Pieter van Musschenbroek lived, gave scientists an easy way to continue their experiments. After rubbing a glass tube with a piece of silk or chamois to generate frictional electricity, they would transmit the electricity to the jar and store it there. In this respect the jar served the same purpose as an electrical bat-

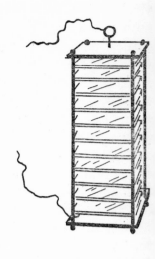

LEYDEN JAR   STORAGE BATTERY—EARLY MODEL

tery. From one jarful scientists could draw electrical power for a whole series of experiments. Up to that time they had only known how to make enough electricity for a single experiment.

In an unexpected way this sidetracked many European scientists from their research. They soon found that they could earn a great deal of money by public exhibitions of electricity. From city to city they traveled, like magicians, performing electrical tricks. They dazzled their audiences by striking long, snapping sparks. They drew objects toward them and forced them away by electrical magnetism. They called on bold onlookers to come forward and receive electrical shocks.

However much the more high-minded scientists frowned on it, this sensational technique raised public interest in Europe to a fever pitch. Later, as an outgrowth of Franklin's electrical research, other scientists took up this practice in America, catching the fancy of the colonists as well.

In the midst of all this furor, Franklin, too, made his first acquaintance with electricity. "In 1746," he later recalled, "being at Boston, I met there with a Dr. Spence, who was lately arrived from Scotland, and show'd me some electric experiments. They were imperfectly perform'd, as he was not very expert; but, being a subject quite new to me, they equally suppris'd and pleased me."

When Franklin returned from Boston to Philadelphia, he eagerly told of his experience before a meeting of the American Philosophical Society, the offspring of his earlier club, the Junto. Immediately interested, the group could not conduct their own experiments because they had no equipment with which to work. Soon, however, Franklin's friend in London, Peter Collinson, sent them a tube of green glass, about three feet long and thick enough to permit an easy grasp. At the same time Collinson outlined a series of experiments he thought worth trying.

As the leader of the group and the only one who had seen electricity in action, Franklin had first turn at trying out the tube. His imagination captured by the vision of exploring a whole scientific sphere of tempting and unbroken trails, he thrilled to this privilege. "I eagerly seized the opportunity," he wrote, "of repeating what I had seen at Boston; and, by much practice, acquired great readiness in performing those, also, which we had an account of from England, adding a number of new ones."

To his distress, however, Franklin's research attracted crowds of curious visitors who shattered his privacy and peace, his house "continually full, for some time, with people who came to see these new wonders." At last he decided to turn over the burden of miracle man, so to speak, to some of his scientific friends. From a local glass manufacturer he ordered a number of glass tubes similar to his own. These he gave to his demonstrators, along with instructions in their proper use and sample lectures the men could follow in their public appearances.

Up and down the colonial seaboard Franklin's friends roamed, drawing large audiences eager to see electricity perform its strange wonders. Like their European predecessors, they earned a comfortable income by their travels, with the little green glass tubes as their chief stock-in-trade.

From their work, too, sprang at least one scientific improvement. At first they could electrify the tube only by vigorous hand rubbing with a piece of buckskin on one side of the tube. Seeking a way to ease the physical

Newport, March 16. 1752.

Notice is hereby given to the Curious,

That at the C O U R'T - H O U S E, in the Council-Chamber, is now to be exhibited, and continued from Day to Day, for a Week or two ;

A COURSE of EXPERIMENTS, on the newly-discovered

Electrical FIRE :

Containing, not only the most curious of those that have been made and published in *Europe,* but a considerable Number of new Ones lately made in *Philadelphia* ; to be accompanied with methodical L E C T U R E S on the Nature and Properties of that wonderful Element.

By *Ebenezer Kinnersley.*

LECTURE I.

I. OF Electricity in General, giving some Account of the Discovery of it.

II. That the Electric Fire is a real Element, and different from those heretofore known and named, and *collected* out of other Matter (not created) by the Friction of Glass, &c.

III. That it is an extreamly subtile Fluid.

IV. That it doth not take up any perceptible Time in passing thro' large Portions of Space.

V. That it is intimately mixed with the Substance of all the other Fluids and Solids of our Globe.

VI. That our Bodies at all Times contain enough of it to set a House on Fire.

VII. That tho' it will fire inflammable Matters, itself has no sensible Heat.

VIII. That it differs from common Matter, in this ; its Parts do not mutually attract, but mutually repel each other.

IX. That it is strongly attracted by all other Matter.

X. An artificial Spider, animated by the Electric Fire, so as to act like a live One.

XI. A Shower of Sand, which rises again as fast as it falls.

XII. That common Matter in the Form of Points attracts this Fire more strongly than in any other Form.

XIII. A Leaf of the most weighty of Metals suspended in the Air, as is said of *Mahomet's* Tomb.

XIV. An Appearance like Fishes swimming in the Air.

XV. That this Fire will live in Water, a River not being sufficient to quench the smallest Spark of it.

XVI. A Representation of the Sensitive Plant.

XVII. A Representation of the seven Planets, shewing a probable Cause of their keeping their due Distances from each other, and from the Sun in the Center.

XVIII. The Salute repulsed by the Ladies Fire ; or Fire darting from a Ladies Lips, so that she may defy any Person to salute her.

XIX. Eight musical Bells rung by an electrified Phial of Water.

XX. A Battery of eleven Guns discharged by Fire issuing out of a Person's Finger.

LECTURE II.

I. A Description and Explanation of Mr. *Muschenbrock's* wonderful Bottle.

II. The amazing Force of the Electric Fire in passing thro' a Number of Bodies at the same Instant.

III. An Electric Mine sprung.

IV. Electrified Money, which scarce any Body will take when offer'd to them.

V. A Piece of Money drawn out of a Person's Mouth in spite of his Teeth ; yet without touching it, or offering him the least Violence.

VI. Spirits kindled by Fire darting from a Lady's Eyes (without a Metaphor).

VII. Various Representations of Lightning, the Cause and Effects of which will be explained by a more probable Hypothesis than has hitherto appeared, and some useful Instructions given, how to avoid the Danger of it : How to secure Houses, Ships, &c. from being hurt by its destructive Violence.

VIII. The Force of the Electric Spark, making a fair Hole thro' a Quire of Paper.

IX. Metal melted by it (tho' without any Heat) in less than a thousandth Part of a Minute.

X. Animals killed by it instantaniously.

XI. Air issuing out of a Bladder set on Fire by a Spark from a Person's Finger, and burning like a Volcano.

XII. A few Drops of electrified cold Water let fall on a Person's Hand, supplying him with Fire sufficient to kindle a burning Flame with one of the Fingers of his other Hand.

XIII. A Sulphurous Vapour kindled into Flame by Fire issuing out of a cold Apple.

XIV. A curious Machine acting by means of the Electric Fire, and playing Variety of Tunes on eight musical Bells.

XV. A Battery of eleven Guns discharged by a Spark, after it has passed through ten Foot of Water.

As the Knowledge of Nature tends to enlarge the human Mind, and give us more noble, more grand, and exalted Ideas of the AUTHOR of Nature, and if well pursu'd, seldom fails producing something useful to Man, 'tis hoped these Lectures may be tho't worthy of Regard & Encouragement.

☞ *Tickets to be had at the House of the Widow* Allen, *in* Thames Street, *next Door to Mr.* John Tweed'y's. *Price* Thirty Shillings *each Lecture. The Lectures to begin each Day precisely at* Three *o'Clock in the Afternoon*

BROADSIDE ANNOUNCING THE FIRST LECTURE ON
ELECTRICITY, NEWPORT: JAMES FRANKLIN, 1752

strain, one of the group, silversmith Philip Syng, invented a machine a little like a grindstone. To one end of an axle he fastened the glass tube to be electrically charged. The other end of the axle was shaped into a handle. Holding the buckskin against the glass, he could turn the tube around by means of the handle. Thus he filled the tube with electricity with much less time and trouble.

Among his disciples Franklin had recruited his neighbor, Ebenezer Kinnersley, destined to become his closest co-worker and fast friend. A minister by profession, Kinnersley had long devoted his spare time to the study of science. Knowing he was out of work, Franklin urged him to conduct some electrical demonstrations. Kinnersley quickly became one of the most popular of the performers, lecturing even as far off as the West Indies.

Although this work, of course, solved his financial problems, it meant much more to him than fortune-hunting. Extremely intelligent and capable at research, he made a number of original discoveries, which he described in letters to Franklin. Often, when he returned from a trip, he and Franklin carried out experiments together. For many years he shared Franklin's fame and glory as an electrical scientist. Even after Kinnersley's reputation faded, Franklin credited him for his contributions, remaining his firm friend throughout life.

Meanwhile, free of curious intruders, Franklin

plunged deep into his new researches. Now he could write to Peter Collinson: "I never was before engaged in any study that so totally engrossed my attention and my time as this has lately done." Before long he had reached a few basic conclusions on the subject.

First he questioned whether friction really created electricity. Instead, he believed that all matter contained electricity in a natural state, and that rubbing objects together merely transferred it from one to the other. This explanation he called the one-fluid theory of electricity, inventing the terms *positive* and *negative*, or *plus* and *minus* to identify its elements. Franklin's analysis, much more accurate than the idea of frictional electricity divided into vitreous and resinous energy, came very close to our modern understanding of the electrical make-up of matter. Today scientists claim that matter is composed of positive and negative particles of electricity known as electrons and protons. When a substance contains an excess of protons, we say it is charged positively. When it contains surplus electrons, we say it is charged negatively.

To prove his one-fluid theory of electricity, Franklin conducted a series of interesting experiments. His pioneer use of the terms *plus* and *minus* also came about through these electrical tests. One in particular which he performed called for human guinea pigs, so he asked three of his friends to help him. For the sake of the story, let us call them John, Jim, and Joe.

In preparation for the experiment Franklin had built

two wooden platforms covered with wax insulation. John and Jim stepped up onto the platform, Joe standing a little distance away.

Here enters the glass tube again. John, chosen to electrify the tube, rubbed it with a piece of silk.

Then Jim reached over and touched the glass tube, receiving into his body a charge of electricity. Both John and Jim now had enough electrical energy in their bodies to cause small, light articles to move toward them.

When Joe walked toward John or Jim, he received a shock, since these two men were filled with more than their normal amount of electricity.

Finally, when John and Jim touched shoulders at once, a large spark crackled between them. The store of electricity within them had now returned to normal.

Through this experiment and several others, Franklin finally discovered, as we have said, that by rubbing two objects together, man does not make electricity, but merely transmits it from one object to another in large or small amounts. And he and his co-workers concluded that John and Jim were electrized positively, or plus, Joe negatively, or minus.

In the course of his research Franklin also discovered that pointed objects proved helpful "both in drawing off and throwing off the electrical fire." From the ceiling he hung a cork attached to a silk thread. Then he held an electrified metal ball close to the cork. The cork jumped back. Close to the metal ball he now

58

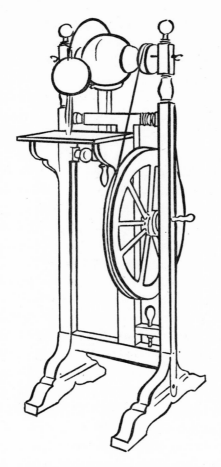

FRANKLIN'S ELECTRICAL
MACHINE (AT FRANKLIN
INSTITUTE)

placed the blade of a bodkin, a needlelike instrument used to punch holes in cloth and leather. As the needle withdrew electrical energy from the metal ball, the cork moved toward it. When he used a bodkin with a blunt point, he noticed that he had to bring the needle very close to the ball before the cork would move toward it.

If this experiment were conducted in the dark, Franklin said, a spark like a firefly would appear at the point of the blade as the bodkin approached the electrified ball, even before the two objects really met. The less sharp the point of the tool, the nearer it had to come to the ball to create the flash of light. In Franklin's mind this little spark struck fire in a new vision, the first glimmering of the lightning rod to come.

As these experiments progressed, Franklin and his friends invented a number of new kinds of electrical equipment. One of these, the first storage battery, appeared in the winter of 1749. For electrical plates they used eleven pieces of ordinary window glass about six by eight inches in size, covering both sides of each pane with sheets of lead. Roughly corresponding to the lead plates of modern storage batteries, these were hung the long way on silk cords about two inches apart. To attach them to the cords, Franklin made heavy hooks of lead wire. By fastening the wire transmitting the electrical charge from the giving side of one plate to the receiving side of the other plate, he charged the entire battery with frictional electricity as easily as he could charge a single pane of glass. From the battery extended two long wires which made it possible to use the stored-up electricity for various experiments. Sometimes, as we shall see, these pioneers in electrical science amused themselves by performing various electrical tricks with the help of their storage battery.

Gradually Franklin had accumulated the wealth of information which led him naturally to his next discovery, the lightning rod, most famous of all his contributions to our understanding of electricity.

CHAPTER SIX

Is Lightning Electricity?

✦✦

IF FRANKLIN HAD never accomplished anything else, his name would probably have lived on into our own times for his lightning rod alone. For the lightning rod could not be counted among his many "contrivances." In proving electricity and lightning one and the same, he had completed a study which Carl Van Doren says "must be ranked with the most fundamental as well as the most striking experiments in scientific history." Today we relate his experiment with the kite as an anecdote, almost like the legend of Washington and the cherry tree. But in 1752, Mr. Van Doren points out, "It was something immense, and it gave Franklin the reputation of a wizard, not too much unlike . . . Einstein."

In November, 1749, Franklin put down in his record of electrical experiments his first notes on the comparison of lightning with electricity: "Electrical fluid agrees with lightning in these particulars: 1. Giving light. 2. Colour of the light. 3. Crooked direction. 4. Swift motion. 5. Being conducted by metals. 6. Crack or noise in exploding. 7. Subsisting in water or ice. 8. Rending bodies it passes through. 9. Destroying animals. 10. Melting metals. 11. Firing inflammable substances. 12. Sulphurous smell.—The electric fluid is attracted by points.—We do not know whether this property is in lightning.—But since they agree in all particulars wherein we can already compare them, is it not probable they agree likewise in this? Let the experiment be made."

How eagerly he must have written these last words, "Let the experiment be made." Did Franklin recognize in his new theory the foundations of a landmark in electrical progress? Surely he must have had a feeling that he had stumbled on something really big.

Nevertheless, it look long and careful thought to plan a suitable experiment. Finally, in the summer of 1750, he began his laboratory test. Secluded in his little workshop, he proceeded as usual with the simplest tools: paper, cardboard, sewing needle, brass scales, cord, and a silversmith's punch.

Still grateful to his friend in London, Peter Collinson, who had sent him the glass tube for his first experiments, Franklin wrote to him about this new undertaking:

"I have a large prime conductor, made of several thin sheets of clothier's pasteboard, formed into a tube, near ten feet long and a foot diameter. It is covered with Dutch embossed paper, almost totally gilt. This large metallic surface supports a much greater electrical atmosphere than a rod or iron of fifty times weight would do. It is suspended by silk line."

Continuing his letter, Franklin described the first part of his experiment:

"Take a pair of large brass scales, of two or more feet beam, the cords of the scales being silk. Suspend the beam by a pack-thread from the ceiling, so that the bottom of the scales may be about a foot from the floor; the scales will move round in a circle by the untwisting of the pack-thread. Set the iron punch on the end upon the floor, in such a place as that the scales may pass over it in making their circle; then electrify one scale by applying the wire of a charged phial to it. As they move round, you see that scale draw nigher to the floor, and dip more when it comes over the punch; and if that be placed at a proper distance, the scale will snap and discharge its fire into it."

To understand the meaning of this, Franklin compared his tools to the elements of nature. The scales and tube with their horizontal circular motion represented electrified clouds, slowly untwisting like thunder clouds above the earth. When he set the silversmith's punch upright on the floor, it represented the highest point on a building or mountain. By watching what happened as the scales and tube circled over the punch, he could see "how electrified clouds, passing over hills or high buildings at too great a height to strike, may be attracted lower till within their striking distance."

Franklin wanted, of course, to turn away the fire transmitted by his pasteboard tube, which when charged would "strike, at near two inches distance, a pretty hard stroke, so as to make one's knuckle ache." Here the sewing needle came in. For, he wrote to Collinson, "Let a person standing on the floor present the point of a needle, at twelve or more inches distant from it, and while the needle is so presented, the conductor cannot be charged, the point drawing off the fire as fast as it is thrown on by the electrical globe."

Now Franklin wondered whether the needle could do the same thing after the tube was charged. This worked, too. "Let it be charged, and then present the point at the same distance, and it will suddenly be discharged. In the dark you may see the light on the point, when the experiment is made. And if the person holding the point stands upon wax, he will be electrified by receiving the fire at that distance."

Next he made the test with an unpointed instrument. "Attempt to draw off the electricity with a blunt body, as a bolt of iron round at the end, and smooth (a silversmith's iron punch, inch thick is what I use) and you must bring it within the distance of three inches before you can do it, and then it is done with a stroke and crack. As the pasteboard tube hangs loose on silk lines, when you approach it with the punch-iron, it likewise will move towards the punch, being attracted while it is charged; but if, at the same instant, a point be presented as before, it retires again, for the point discharges it."

Certain now that he must use a sharp point to carry out his purpose, Franklin turned to the most important part of his experiment. Setting the silversmith's punch straight up again on the floor, he arranged the scales and tube in position above it. When he set the needle "on the end of the punch, its point upwards," he found that "the scale, instead of drawing nigh to the punch, and snapping, discharges its fire silently through the point, and rises higher from the punch. . . . And this is constantly observable in these experiments, that the greater the quantity of electricity on the pasteboard tube, the farther it strikes or discharges its fire, and the point likewise will draw off at a still greater distance."

From the action of the little needle, Franklin thus drew his inspiration for a lightning rod to provide protection against fire flashing from the skies. "May not the knowledge of this power of points," he asked, "be of use to mankind in preserving houses, churches, ships, etc., from the stroke of lightning, by directing us to fix on the highest parts of those edifices upright rods of iron made sharp as a needle, and gilt to prevent rusting, and from the foot of those rods a wire down the outside of the building into the ground, or down round one of the shrouds of a ship, and down her side till it reaches the water?"

Through his indoor experiments Franklin had come

at last to the most important question: "If a needle fixed on the punch with its point upright, or even on the floor below the punch, will draw the fire from the scale silently . . . would not these pointed rods probably draw the electrical fire silently out of a cloud before it came nigh enough to strike, and thereby secure us from that most sudden and terrible mischief?"

Only one test could determine the answer, the test of a real lightning rod in a real storm. Franklin laid down his plan for this. "On the top of some high tower or steeple, place a kind of sentry-box, big enough to contain a man and an electrical stand. From the middle of the stand let an iron rod rise and pass bending out of the door, and then upright twenty or thirty feet, pointed very sharp at the end. If the electrical stand be kept clean and dry, a man standing on it when such clouds are passing low might be electrified and afford sparks, the rod drawing fire to him from a cloud."

Franklin did not believe the man would be hurt by this, but to further protect himself from harm, he could "stand on the floor of this box, and now and then bring near to the rod the loop of a wire that has one end fastened to the leads, he holding it by a wax handle; so the sparks, if the rod is electrified, will strike from the rod to the wire and not affect him."

Oddly enough, Franklin himself never performed this final experiment. Perhaps at this point some of his other pressing duties interrupted. For one thing, he believed the success of the test depended largely on the selection of a very high location. Since he could not find a suitable spot in Philadelphia, he finally thought up his experiment with the kite as a substitute. At any rate, it fell upon a French scientist to present the first proof of the lightning-rod theory.

Through Franklin's letters to Peter Collinson and another English friend, Dr. John Mitchel, word of his work had spread abroad. Much impressed, these men read some of his letters before the Royal Society of London, where they had a mixed reception. Many of the members disagreed with Collinson and Mitchel, seeing no significance in Franklin's observations. On one occasion Mitchel sent Franklin word that a paper of his "on the sameness of lightning with electricity . . . had been read, but was laughed at by the connoisseurs."

However, not even the snub of the Royal Society could halt these important investigations. Through the efforts of Dr. John Fothergill of London, Franklin's letters soon appeared in the form of a pamphlet. When Fothergill first suggested having them printed, Peter Collinson took them to Edward Cave, the editor of *Gentleman's Magazine,* to see if he would use them in that publication. Apparently Cave realized that the material was much too valuable for a mere magazine article. Instead he printed the little pamphlet, which contained a preface by Dr. Fothergill. Although it sold well enough to justify five editions, it failed to change the minds of English scientists.

Meanwhile copies of the pamphlet somehow turned

up in France. There Count de Buffon, an outstanding French scientist, read it with great interest. In spite of the very poor translation, he immediately appreciated its importance. Under his encouragement his associate, Thomas-Francois D'Alibard, prepared another version in French. When this new translation, much better than the first, appeared in France in 1752, it made an exciting stir among French scientists. Most enthusiastic of all, Buffon, D'Alibard, and their friend De Lor could hardly wait to carry out Franklin's proposed lightning-rod experiment.

Before they could do so, however, new opposition arose among a group of French scientists headed by Abbé Nollet. A member of the royal family, Nollet had a high reputation in the field of natural philosophy and had set forth some electrical theories of his own which ran opposite to much of Franklin's thought. When he first read the pamphlet, he suspected some of his fellow-countrymen of writing it to discredit him. Finally convinced of its true authorship, he wrote a series of letters to Franklin in defense of his own views. Later these letters, too, appeared in book form.

At first Franklin wanted to reply to Nollet, of course, but soon he thought better of it. As he once wrote to a friend: "I have *never* entered into any controversy in defence of my philosophical opinions; I leave them to take their chance in the world. If they are *right,* truth and experience will support them; if *wrong,* they ought to be *refuted* and *rejected.*"

His supporters in France came to his rescue, with D'Alibard, a member of the French Royal Academy taking the lead as the first to carry out the lightning-rod experiment. In the garden of his home he erected an iron rod about forty feet tall and an inch thick. At the top of this rod he placed a slender piece of brass. To insulate his rod from the ground, he set it up on a wooden stool with three wine bottles for legs.

Now he waited impatiently for a thunderstorm. When it struck, on May 10, 1752, however, D'Alibard was away from his home in the village of Marly, near Paris. Fortunately he had prepared for such an emergency by instructing the local clergyman to take over in his absence.

Upon the approach of the storm, therefore, the minister ran to D'Alibard's garden, the townspeople following at his heels. As the clergyman drew forth the electrical charge, sparks flashed and crackled from the rod. What a gasp of amazement must have risen from his audience!

Quickly he rushed off a detailed account to D'Alibard in Paris. After three days of meditation on the facts, D'Alibard in turn submitted a formal report to the French Royal Academy proclaiming the truth of Franklin's theory. This firmly established Franklin's position throughout the world as a top-ranking scientist, a position strengthened several days later when De Lor, the Parisian friend of D'Alibard, repeated the experiment successfully.

D'Alibard's Garden During the Experiment

But in those days news did not flash around the world with modern speed. Though these experiments secured Franklin's fame, word of their completion traveled slowly. In June, 1752, a whole month after his French friends had proved his theory, Franklin apparently had not yet heard his own success story. For at that time, the record indicates, he finally set out to attempt his substitute experiment with the kite.

In building his kite, he made a cross frame with two light strips of cedar wood. Over this he stretched a large silk handkerchief, which he fastened to the four points of the wooden frame. Ordinarily, of course, a kite is covered with paper, but Franklin used the silk handkerchief instead because paper would never hold up under the rain and wind of a heavy thunderstorm.

After adding the usual tail, loop, and cord, Franklin fastened to the top of the vertical bar of his kite frame a sharply pointed strip of wire about a foot long. To the string which would guide the course of the kite he tied a key and a short strip of silk ribbon, selecting for this purpose a point near which his hand must grasp the cord when he flew the kite.

In planning his experiment, Franklin foresaw that he would have to stand under shelter while flying the kite. "The silk ribbon tied to the cord must not be allowed to get wet. At the same time, however, while one did stand under cover, care must be taken to see that the cord does not touch any portion of the shelter." That, he realized, could neutralize or ground the electrical charge flowing through the kite string.

At last the stormy day arrived. With his twenty-one-year-old son William at his side, Franklin hurried out to a nearby field, heading for the small woodshed halfway across it. When we remember that Franklin had no idea of what had happened in France a short time earlier, we can imagine his excitement and stagefright at that moment. "Am I really correct," he must have

72

wondered, "in thinking and believing that lightning and electricity are one and the same substance?" As far as he knew, the events of the next few minutes must prove whether his theory was true or false!

Tensely he hoisted his kite and waited as the thunderclouds passed overhead. The minutes sped by. No sign of electricity appeared. Anxiously Franklin studied the rolling clouds. Surely that last threatening one would strike! But no, it moved on and disappeared.

His hopes falling, Franklin looked back at the cord again. Suddenly he noticed several strands separate, each standing out very erectly. Quickly moving his hand, he placed his knuckles near the key. Then the sparks came! Weak and slow at first, they gathered strength as the kite string got wetter and wetter. Soon they shot forth in such rapid succession that Franklin collected a generous supply of electrical energy in his glass tubes.

When the storm ended, Franklin returned home a happy man indeed. Now he knew the truth for certain: lightning and electricity sprang from a single force of nature.

On the other side of the ocean, word of the lightning-rod experiments in France soon reached the ears of scientists in London. Later Franklin learned how this turned the tide of English opinion in his favor. "Dr. Wright, an English physician when at Paris, wrote to a friend, who was of the Royal Society, an account of the high esteem my experiments were in among the learned

FRANKLIN'S FAMOUS KITE EXPERIMENT

abroad, and of their wonder that my writings had been so little noticed in England. The society, on this, resum'd the consideration of the letters that had been read to them; and the celebrated Dr. Watson drew up a summary account of them, and of all I had afterwards sent to England on the subject, which he accompanied with some praise of the writer. This summary was then printed in their Transactions."

And so, after all their doubting laughter, English scientists proceeded to repeat the lightning-rod experiment for the third time, carrying it out as successfully as D'Alibard and De Lor. Once convinced of their mistake, the Royal Society of London repaid Franklin graciously for their previous hasty judgment. "Without my having made any application for that honour," he marveled, "they chose me a member, and voted that I should be excus'd the customary payments, which would have amounted to twenty-five guineas; and ever since have given me their Transactions gratis." To add to the compliment, they awarded Franklin "the gold medal of Sir Godfrey Copley for the year 1753, the delivery of which was accompanied by a very handsome speech of the president, Lord Macclesfield."

Thus in England itself rose the wave of tribute to Franklin which rolled on to ever greater heights until it swept over colonial shores at last.

CHAPTER SEVEN

Using Electricity for
Fun and Otherwise

❖❖

EAGER AS EVER to make new knowledge serve humanity, Franklin lost little time in suggesting a practical application for his electrical discoveries. In *Poor Richard's Almanac* he soon printed instructions to readers on how to protect their homes and farms from the ravages of lightning with the use of pointed rods of steel or iron.

A few months after carrying out his experiment with the kite, he erected a lightning rod on his own house, not only for protection but also to provide natural electricity for his experiments. For ordinary use he recommended a rod about six feet long, tapering in thickness from one-half inch at one end to a sharp point at the other, the point gilded to prevent rusting. However, his own lightning rod was much longer, extending nine feet from the chimney instead of the usual three or four.

The general plan included a second inch-thick rod of steel or iron, this one about ten or twelve feet long. Erecting it about ten feet away from the house, the family drove this rod deep into the soil until it rose only about three feet above ground level. Then they connected the two rods with a length of wire or several additional lengths of rod soldered together with molten lead. Should lightning strike, the electricity would pass from the chimney rod through the wire into the rod beside the house, protecting lives and property against fire. For unusually large houses Franklin suggested the use of several lightning rods, all connected by a single wire.

In setting up his own lightning rod, Franklin used a slightly different plan. From the bottom of the rod attached to the chimney he ran a wire through a glass tube in the roof and on downward through the well of the staircase, fastened at the other end to the iron spear of a small pump. On the staircase opposite his bedroom door, he split the wire and strung between the two ends a silk thread about six inches long. Hanging a bell at each end of the wire, he suspended a small brass ball from the silk thread between them.

Whenever thunderclouds passed overhead, the brass ball would swing back and forth, making the bells ring, announcing that the wire was discharging electrical current. Hearing the signal, Franklin would rush out and charge one of his electrical tubes for use in further experiments.

FRANKLIN'S BELLS RINGING BY ELECTRICITY

One night Franklin heard a loud sputtering noise from the hall. Startled, he ran to his bedroom door. The brass ball, instead of vibrating as usual between the two bells, remained motionless at an equal distance from each, the electrical discharge flashing in quick sparks from bell to bell, making now and then, said Franklin, "a continued, dense, white stream, seemingly as large as my finger, whereby the whole staircase en-lightened as with sunshine, so that one might see to pick up a pin."

For years Franklin's lightning bells tinkled their electrical messages in his home, fascinating visitors even when silent. However, the lightning rod itself did not at first win much support among the colonists. Some people, of course, poked fun at it as at every new invention. Others criticized it out of superstitious fears. Since they believed lightning was a symbol of God's anger toward sinful men, they felt human beings should not interfere with it. Only after a number of years, when stories spread about homes or churches saved by a lightning rod during a storm, did people recognize the importance of this invention. Franklin himself re-ceived reports of five different buildings in the colonies which had escaped damage by lightning only through the use of the lightning rod.

In Europe, in spite of the enthusiasm of its scientists for Franklin's electrical discoveries, the general public reacted to the lightning rod in much the same way as the colonists. Some twenty years after Franklin's inven-tion, a storm of controversy arose in England over the comparative merits of pointed and blunt-tipped light-ning rods. At a place called Purfleet the British Board of Ordnance maintained large powder magazines. Anx-ious to protect the storage buildings against lightning, they applied for advice on the problem to the Royal Society, which promptly appointed a committee of five men, including Franklin, to visit Purfleet and study the question.

Among their recommendations the committee suggested the installation of lightning rods. Four of them agreed in urging the use of the sharp-pointed rod Franklin had introduced, but the fifth member, Benjamin Wilson, violently opposed them, supporting a rod designed with a blunt tip. When the Board of Ordnance accepted the majority opinion, Wilson proved a poor loser, writing several pamphlets in which he attacked Franklin and the committee.

True to his principles, Franklin refused to defend his viewpoint. Wilson, on the other hand, gained a powerful supporter in King George III. Just about the time the debate reached its peak, the colonists launched the American Revolution. To the king, the pointed lightning rod now became a hateful reminder of his rebel colonists. Unfortunately, nature came to his aid when lightning struck one of the powder magazines in Purfleet which had been equipped with Franklin's lightning rod. Although the building was undamaged, the king ordered all the pointed rods at Purfleet removed and replaced with knob-tipped ones.

In spite of his hasty action, the king had a guilty conscience in the matter. To gain reassurance of the wisdom of his order, he commanded the head of the Royal Society, Sir John Pringle, to approve what he had done. Sir John, a firm supporter of Franklin's lightning rod now became a hateful reminder of his rebel to the king's request. Instantly fired from the office of royal physician, he was soon removed, also, under the king's pressure, from his presidency of the Royal Society. Thus he sacrificed his whole career for the sake of scientific truth.

Along with all its difficulties and conflicts, Franklin's electrical work provided him and his friends with various stunts, one of which gave them many a laugh on the tyrannical king. To play this joke, called "The Conspirators," they needed a picture of George III. Removing the portrait from the frame, they cut it down about two inches all around. This two-inch border strip of the portrait they pasted on the back of the glass. Then they filled in the rest of the glass back and the same portion of the front with gilt paint. Over the gilded square on the front of the glass they pasted the center part of the portrait. Although part of the portrait was on the front of the glass and part on the back, it looked exactly as it had before. Now they changed the appearance slightly by placing a small movable gold crown on the king's head, after which they replaced the picture in the frame.

Having charged the crown full of electricity, the scientists carried out their prank by urging an unsuspecting colonist to remove the crown with one hand, at the same time placing his other hand on a portion of the gilded frame. Much to his amazement, the victim, of course, received a shock for his attempted "disloyalty."

Sometimes they got a number of people to hold hands

while the first tried to remove the crown from the king's portrait. Naturally, the shock received by the leader then passed through the whole group of "conspirators," so named because of their attempt to uncrown the king.

To further confuse the audience, the demonstrator would finally remove the crown himself without getting any shock, simply by placing one hand on an ungilded portion of the frame. Smiling broadly, he would tease the puzzled onlookers with this proof of his greater loyalty to the crown!

After their first busy winter of electrical experimentation, Franklin and his assistants took time out for a spring picnic. During the summer months they could not expect to carry on their work because warm weather made it difficult to generate frictional electricity. Therefore, they made the picnic an occasion for a grand review of all their findings up to that point.

The picnic day rose bright and sunny. Off to the banks of the Schuylkill River near Philadelphia they carted their food supplies and scientific equipment. Soon they stretched out on the grass, eating and planning their program.

As one of their first tricks, they sent an electrical charge clear across the river, setting afire a spoonful of alcohol on the opposite bank. Into the ground at the water's edge on each side of the river they drove an iron rod about three feet long. Attached to the rod near the spoonful of alcohol hung a heavy piece of wire with a small knot at one end. This wire they bent downward so that it would touch the alcohol. From the handle of the spoon extended another length of wire which stretched right over the width of the river, supported by the rope ordinarily used for ferry traffic, tied at the picnic bank around the neck of the electrical tube.

When the iron rod erected near the electrical tube received a spark, this electric current, conducted by the water, charged the rod on the opposite shore. Then the second rod sent forth a spark which ignited the alcohol in the spoon nearby, amidst astonished gasps from the guests who were standing by, pop-eyed.

At last the scientists introduced the most interesting feature of any picnic program: the food. However, even

ELECTRICAL PICNIC: ALCOHOL BEING LIT

in serving the eats, they demonstrated the wonders of electricity. Having brought the turkey along alive, they now slaughtered it by electric shock. Franklin had tried this method of killing fowl and claimed it left the meat far more tender than the old-fashioned ax. Ordinarily he used six large electric tubes charged with current to perform the electrocution. This time he fastened a chain around the turkey's leg and extended it to the battery. Then he raised the wings of the turkey over its head until they touched, so that the charge would strike hardest at the head. The electrical charge killed the turkey instantly. After preparing the lifeless bird in the usual way, the cooks roasted it over a fire started by an electrical spark.

Of course, all the picnickers exclaimed over the delicious flavor of the turkey. Their appetites sharpened by the day's activities, they readily accepted the claim of their hosts that the electricity had done the trick. However, they had no doubt selected a fine turkey in the first place, whose meat would have tasted almost as sweet and tender no matter how they prepared it.

In celebration of the occasion they drank toasts to the outstanding electrical scientists of England, France, Holland, and Germany. Served in small electrified tumblers of thin glass, the toasts touched off electrical shocks on the drinkers' lips. If anyone were not clean-shaven, however, or accidentally breathed on the wine, he might not receive any shock from his glass.

To wind up the party, they fired a farewell salute

from a small cannon set off with an electrical spark. With much noise and laughter, they finally gathered up their belongings and started home again.

In his demonstrations of the wonders of electricity, things did not always go as well for Franklin as they had on this delightful spring picnic. Careful as he was, he experienced a number of electrical accidents. One Christmas, for example, in electrocuting a turkey before an audience of friends, he got his equipment mixed up and applied the current to himself instead of to the bird. In his account of the incident, he described his sensation as a "universal blow from head to foot . . . followed by a violent quick trembling in the trunk, which gradually went off in a few seconds." He did not see the flash nor hear the pistol-like shot which the onlookers reported to him. Neither did he feel the stroke on his hand, though he "afterwards found it had raised a swelling there the bigness of half a swan shot or pistol bullet." For the rest of the evening his arms and back felt numb, his breastbone remaining sore for a week.

Franklin laughed at his blunder, comparing it with that of the Irishman who tried to steal a keg of blasting powder and ended by making a hole in the cask with a hot iron. However, he must have shivered at the thought of "what the consequences would be if such a shock were taken through the head."

A short time later Franklin had a second mishap. Because of a widespread belief that electric shock helped paralysis victims, such patients often came to him for treatment. On one such occasion, Franklin afterward wrote to his friend Jan Ingenhousz, he "had a patient . . . whose friends brought him to receive some electric shocks." In order to discharge the shock to the whole group at once, he suggested that they hold hands. Filling two large jars with electricity for the purpose, he set off the charge.

Again, however, he unfortunately got things twisted so that he, instead of his patients, received the shock. As in his other experience, he "neither saw the flash, heard the report, nor felt the stroke." In fact, when he came to, he did not believe he had already discharged the jars, "but on trial found it true."

At first neither he nor the others could understand why he had been knocked down by the shock. He soon realized, however, how this had happened. In preparing to apply the charge, he had taken his position "inadvertently under an iron hook which hung from the ceiling down to within two inches" of his head. When the electricity passed through his body, it made him jump, thus striking his head on the hook and falling unconscious. The bump from the hook caused a small swelling on his head which hurt for a few days, but he did not notice "any other effect good or bad."

A much more dangerous accident occurred when Franklin conducted an experiment to see how a charge of electricity would affect a small quantity of powdered amber. He had two questions in mind. First, would the charge melt the amber? Second, if so, would the amber harden again?

Into the center of a small glass tube he rammed the powdered amber. Having left the ends of the tube open, he now slipped into each a length of wire connected to an electrified jar. When he released the electricity, the glass blew up, the fragments flying in all directions. Bits of glass struck Franklin's face with tremendous force. Had his eyes been hit, he might have lost his sight. Fortunately, the shattered glass only cut his lip and stunned him for the moment.

Not one to give up an idea, Franklin repeated the experiment, this time using a cardboard tube as a safeguard in the event of a second explosion. Had Franklin and his helpers stopped to worry about the risks they ran in conducting their electrical research, they would have hesitated at each experiment, since all held unknown dangers. For example, the lightning-rod test, performed successfully in France and England, killed a Swedish scientist. How lucky for us that the others carried on!

Quite in contrast to this disregard for personal injury to themselves from electricity, they gave great attention to its possible healing effects on others. Most of Franklin's experiments on paralytic victims occurred in 1751, only five years after his first experience with electricity at Dr. Spence's Boston demonstration.

Later Franklin wrote to Sir John Pringle, then England's royal physician, explaining how it started.

"When the newspapers made mention of great cures performed in Italy and Germany by means of electricity, a number of paralytics were brought to me from different parts of Pennsylvania and the neighboring provinces, to be electrized, which I did for them at their request."

With the patient seated in a chair, on an electrical stool, Franklin drew "a number of large strong sparks from all parts of the affected limb or side." Then he would charge two six-gallon glass jars and release the electricity into the paralyzed areas, repeating the treatment three times a day.

Encouraging signs appeared very quickly. The shock brought "an immediate greater sensible warmth in the lame limbs that had received the stroke than in the others; and the next morning the patients usually related that they had in the night felt a pricking sensation in the flesh of the paralytic limbs; and would sometimes show a number of small red spots which they supposed were occasioned by those prickings." Often a man "who could not the first day lift the lame hand from off his knee, would the next day raise it four or five inches, the third day higher; and on the fifth day was able, but with a feeble, languid motion, to take off his hat."

This miraculous improvement, Franklin wrote, sometimes made the patients "hope a perfect cure." But alas! After the fifth day, progress generally halted. Then the patient, discouraged, usually went home and soon lapsed into his original condition. Franklin, carefully examining the facts, did not overlook the possibility that "the apparent temporary advantage might arise from the exercise in the patient's journey, and coming daily to my house, or from the spirits given by the hope of success, enabling them to exert more strength in moving their limbs."

In reporting his findings, Franklin suggested to Sir John that others might be able to follow up this matter. "Perhaps some permanent advantage might have been obtained if the electric shocks had been accompanied with proper medicine and regimen, under the direction of a skillful physician. It may be, too, that a few great strokes, as given in my method, may not be so proper as many small ones." At any rate, this study required more concentration than Franklin could allow for it in his busy schedule of science and politics.

In addition to all this work, Franklin now received a barrage of correspondence from people far and wide who had come to look upon him as an authority in electrical matters. After his successful experiments with lightning, the volume of letters increased, many requesting advice on protection against lightning strokes.

To these inquiries Franklin replied with detailed suggestions. Of course, anyone could just dash under the bed or hide in a closet until the storm passed, but such a person would hardly come to Franklin for help. The methods he recommended involved both greater detail and greater dignity.

During a storm the safest place was the middle of

the room, away from chimneys, mirrors, and gilt-framed pictures. Here Franklin suggested sitting on a chair with the feet resting on another chair. If a person wished still greater protection, he could place on the floor under his chair two or three mattresses, folded double. This obviously called for acrobatic skill. Franklin's favorite technique, a hammock suspended by silk cords in the middle of the room, offered the greatest protection. However, he pointed out the extreme care necessary to hang it at an exactly equal distance from the four walls of the room and between floor and ceiling.

Whether or not these precautions ever saved anyone we do not know today. But anyone who went to the trouble of trying them certainly deserved to reap such a reward.

There is little doubt that Franklin's achievements in the electrical field brought him his greatest fame. His new theory of electricity and its relation to lightning, along with the invention of the lightning rod, were outstanding milestones in his career as an inventor and scientist. He coined many words relating to electricity which are in common use today, such as *brush, non-conductor, armature,* and *battery.* Indeed, little of that science as it existed in his day escaped his keen mind.

Scores of scientists followed Franklin with further discoveries in electricity, many unquestionably far more brilliant in that particular field than he. But few, if any, could claim the unique distinction that was

Franklin's. Without benefit of formal scientific training, he made basic discoveries which turned into foundation stones for a monumental science then in its cradle stage. For this, could we not justly call Franklin the father of electricity?

CHAPTER EIGHT

Sea Interests

◇◇◇

THROUGHOUT HIS LIFE, whatever the immediate project under his attention, Franklin never lost his love for the sea. At an early age, as you will remember, he dreamed of running off to sea. When his father talked him out of this ambition, he little suspected how many ocean voyages life held in store for the restless boy. Franklin's first opportunity for a trip abroad came when he was eighteen. Governor Keith of Pennsylvania sent him to England. Between that time and the end of his life he completed eight round trips across the Atlantic, a remarkable record in those days of rugged sailing conditions and snail-pace ships.

Like all other elements of nature, the sea and its workings attracted his curiosity and led him into many experiments with various aspects of its behavior. Although he never carried any of these through to the complete success of his investigations in heating and electricity, he made a number of contributions to marine science. His two major studies in this field centered on the effect of oil on water and the peculiar qualities of the Gulf Stream.

Have you ever heard anyone speak of calming down an angry friend as "pouring oil on troubled waters"? This phrase has come down through the centuries in all languages. Surely Franklin had heard it even as a small boy, but like most of us in our daily speech, never took the meaning of the expression seriously. In his wide reading as a young man, he came upon a story by the Greek historian, Pliny, of how sailors would smooth a choppy sea by pouring oil on the waves. Could oil actually calm real "troubled waters"? Franklin, always weighing scientific truth against superstition, doubted it. As he wrote to a friend many years later, the story didn't ring quite true.

If Franklin smiled a little at Pliny's claim, he afterward fully acknowledged his mistake. In 1757, during one of his ocean voyages, he saw for the first time an incident which made him think Pliny had told the truth. Sailing in a fleet of ships, he "observed the wakes of two of the ships to be remarkably smooth, while all the others were ruffled by the wind, which blew fresh." Finally he could not contain his curiosity and asked the captain to explain this freak of nature. As though he thought the question very stupid, the captain answered, "The cooks have I suppose been just emptying their greasy water through the scuppers, which has greased the sides of those ships a little."

Ridiculous as this sounded, Franklin could not think of a better reason. In his mind he turned the incident over again and again, at the same time recalling what he had read in Pliny. To determine the truth, he "resolved to make some experiment of the effect of oil on water" at the first opportunity. But he had not yet had a chance to do so when, five years later, he saw another example of this remarkable power of oil.

This time his ship stopped at the Azores. As it neared the port one warm evening, the passengers opened the

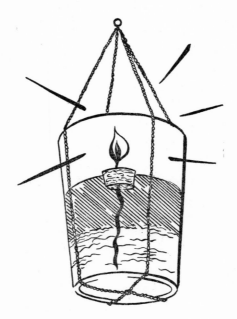

ITALIAN LAMP

94

windows to the fresh air. While the breeze made the cabin more comfortable, it blew out the candles as well. Franklin wanted the cool breeze, but he also wanted candlelight to read by. He kept both comforts by building an "Italian lamp."

Using an ordinary drinking glass, he filled the bottom third with water and the middle third with oil. On the surface of the oil he floated a wick made of a piece of wire attached to some cork to keep it from sinking. The top third of the glass he left empty, so that the sides could protect the flame. After fastening several wires around the glass, he hung it from the ceiling of his cabin.

As he stood a few steps away and examined his handiwork, Franklin noticed that the surface of the oil remained exceptionally smooth, while the water beneath it rose and dipped every time the ship rocked or swayed. Again Franklin turned to a shipmate for help. This man, a former sea captain and now a fellow-passenger, assured him that the construction of the lamp brought about "an effect of the same kind with that of oil, put on water to smooth it," a custom often practiced by fishermen in Bermuda, he explained, "when they would strike fish which they could not see if the surface of the water was ruffled by the wind."

Perhaps suspecting Franklin's disbelief, this friendly old captain told Franklin about other places where seamen made use of oil in the same way. At the mouth of the river leading to the Lisbon docks, he said, the surf boiled dangerously over a sand bar. Often when fishermen sailed from that port, they would pour several bottles of oil over this surf, thus quieting the water enough for them to get their boats through safely. From another passenger on the ship, a Rhode Island colonist, Franklin learned that whenever whaling ships lay anchored at Newport, the harbor remained smooth and peaceful. Everyone believed that the whale oil oozing through the ships' sides from chunks of blubber and leaky barrels performed this curious change on the face of the water.

Franklin could hardly wait to get back home to Philadelphia, where he now built a second hanging lamp purely for test purposes. At first he could make little progress with this new study. However, he persisted in his experiments, gradually working out methods of trial on a larger scale than the lamp permitted. Finally, during one of his stays in England, some encouraging signs appeared.

In his autobiography he tells how one day, in the park at Clapham, he noticed the pond turn rough under a strong wind. Quickly he "fetched a cruet of oil and dropped a little of it on the water . . . saw it spread itself with surprising swiftness upon the surface." When the waves did not subside, he realized he had chosen the wrong side of the pond. There the waves were heaviest, and the wind blew the oil back up on dry ground. Sure enough, when he repeated the test at the other side of the pond, where the waves started to rise, he met with success. "The oil, though not more than a teaspoonful, produced an instant calm over a space several yards square which spread amazingly and extended itself gradually till it reached the lee-side, making all that quarter of the pond, perhaps half an acre, as smooth as a looking-glass."

Now Franklin had to agree with Pliny and with his shipboard friends that oil indeed smoothed ruffled waters, although he could not find the reason. From that time forth he carried a special kind of cane with a little hollow built into it to hold a small amount of oil. Wherever he went this enabled him to conduct an experiment should the opportunity arise. Because of this new habit, he once created an amusing episode at a London garden party.

The host of the gathering, Lord Shelbourne, had invited many well-known guests, both English and French, among them a number of scientists. After a while the conversation, as often happens, reached a low point. Everyone tried hard to think of something bright or funny to say. Suddenly Franklin, with his ready wit, had an idea. Reaching for his cane, he announced that he had the power to bring calm to rough water!

Instantly the garden hummed with excitement. Questions and dares popped from every mouth. Without a word, Franklin led the way to a brook on the Shelbourne estate. Alongside the brook he halted the procession, himself striding on a few paces further on the up-stream side. With a quick movement he yanked apart the two sections of his cane. Over the water he whirled the one containing the oil, at the same time mumbling some words of make-believe magic.

As the cane sprinkled the oil over the waves, the water settled to a smooth, flat calm. Imagine the shouts of astonishment which rose from the audience nearby! The joke had worked. They all believed Franklin knew a magic charm of some kind. Of course, in revealing the truth, Franklin brought even greater delight to these scientific minds than he could have with magic.

Spurred on by this success, Franklin increased his efforts to solve this mystery of oil. One day he met three European scientists also interested in the subject, a Dutch scientist, Count Bentinck, his captain son, and a Professor Allemand. Eagerly Franklin showed them his little experiment of smoothing water with oil. After watching attentively, the count confided to Franklin that he had received a letter telling how a Dutch ship had been saved during a storm by pouring oil on the sea. He promised to send Franklin a copy of the letter to study.

Warming under this exchange of ideas, Franklin asked the others what they thought of another possibility he had been considering. Often he had read accounts of how ships had difficulty in landing on islands for repairs or medical aid, because of the rough surf that circled the shore. Would it not help in such a situation if the captain had a few barrels of oil on hand? By pouring some oil on one stretch of surf, he could perhaps quiet the water enough to make a safe landing.

Enthusiastic at this suggestion, Captain Bentinck urged Franklin to come to Portsmouth, England, where they could try it out. In October, 1773, they made the trip. Captain Bentinck arranged for the use of a long-boat and a barge, and on the first windy day they made the experiment. "The long-boat was anchored about a quarter of a mile from the shore; part of the company were landed behind the point (a place more sheltered from the sea) who came round and placed themselves opposite to the long-boat, where they might observe the surf and note if any change occurred in it upon using the oil. Another party in the barge plied to windward of the long-boat as far from her as she was from the shore, making trips of about half a mile each, pouring oil continually out of a large stone bottle through a hole in the cork somewhat bigger than a goose-quill."

In spite of their high hopes for the idea, the experiment did not prove completely successful, "for no material difference was observed in the height or force of the surf upon the shore." Nevertheless, the people in the long-boat "could observe a tract of smoothed water, the whole of the distance in which the barge poured the oil, and gradually spreading in breadth towards the long-boat." Even this part of the surf did not turn altogether calm, Franklin admitted, but at least "its surface was not roughened by the wrinkles or smaller waves before mentioned, and none or very few white caps (or waves whose tops turn over in foam) appeared in that whole space." What a thrill Franklin must have felt when "a wherry that came round the point under sail, in her way to Portsmouth, seemed to turn into that tract of choice and to use it from end to end as a piece of turnpike road."

To some extent Franklin could understand the reasons for the partial failure, though perhaps they did not lessen his disappointment. In summing up his impressions, he compared the motion of waves to that of a pendulum, which will continue to swing long after the force which set it moving has ceased operating. Thus, "though oil spread on an agitated sea may weaken the push of the wind on those waves whose surfaces are covered by it . . . yet a considerable time, or a distance through which they will take time to move, may be necessary to make the effect sensible on any shore in a diminution of the surf; for we know that when wind ceases suddenly, the waves it has raised do not suddenly subside but settle gradually."

Therefore, Franklin believed, no one could expect waves to be instantly flattened by oil. "The motion they have received will for some time continue; and if the shore is not far distant, they arrive there so soon that their effect upon it will not be visibly diminished."

From these conclusions Franklin, never defeated, proposed a plan for greater perfection of the experiment. "If we had begun our operations at a greater distance, the effect might have been more sensible. And perhaps we did not pour oil in sufficient quantity. Future experiments may determine this."

But these future experiments he left to other scientists. By this time, on the eve of the American Revolution, he had little leisure for experiments. Also, perhaps, he had just about exhausted his curiosity in the matter. At any rate, he had succeeded in recalling to the attention of the world a gift of nature which could stand men at sea in good stead. This it has done more than ever since steamships started converting from coal to oil for fuel. Although Franklin did not discover this trick—though many people think so, since the ancients knew all about it—he certainly gave it new life.

Meanwhile Franklin had become interested in another problem of the maritime field, the nature of the Gulf Stream. In 1769, as deputy postmaster-general of the colonies, he learned of a peculiar complaint made by the Lords of the Treasury of London to the Boston Board of Customs. Apparently the mail-bearing packet boats sailing between Falmouth, England, and New York took almost two weeks longer than merchant ships carrying heavier cargo from London to Rhode Island. Small wonder they complained! They sent the mail by packet boats because supposedly they were the fastest commercial vessels afloat at that time. In addition to this, they had a head start on the slower mer-

101

chant ships, since they left from Falmouth while the others had to go further up the Thames River to London.

As an official of the postal system, Franklin had to investigate this perplexing situation. Through this study he came upon another unexplored scientific wonder. In asking advice about the packet-boat problem from Captain Folger, a distant relative, Franklin learned "that the island in which he lives is inhabited chiefly by people concerned in the whale fishery . . . that the whales are found generally near the edges of the Gulph Stream, a strong current so called, which comes out of the Gulph of Florida passing northeasterly along the coast of America, and then turning off most easterly."

These whale fishermen, cruising along the edge of the Gulf Stream, naturally learned more about it than seamen passing through to and from the colonies. They knew "the strength of it when their boats are out in the pursuit of this fish, and happen to get into the stream while the ship is in it, for then they are separated very fast, and would soon lose sight of each other if care were not taken."

Often in crossing the stream the fishermen would meet packet boats ten weeks out from England, "still far from land, and not likely to be in with it for some time, being engaged in that part of the stream that sets directly against them." Why, one would wonder, did they insist on coming by this route? "It is supposed that their fear of Cape Sable shoals, George's Banks or Nantucket shoals, hath induced them to keep so far southward as unavoidably to engage them in the same Gulph Stream, which occasions the length of their voyages, since in a calm it carries them directly back, and though they may have fair winds, yet the current being 60 or 70 miles a day, it is so much subtracted from the way they make through the water."

With this knowledge of the facts, Franklin offered the only sensible recommendation to Anthony Todd, secretary of the British Post Office. He submitted "written directions whereby ships bound from the Banks of Newfoundland to New York may avoid the said stream, and yet be free of danger from the banks and shoals above mentioned." To show how this would shorten packet-boat voyages, he also enclosed a chart of the Gulf Stream drawn by Captain Folger on which he had marked "the dimensions, course and swiftness of the stream from its first coming out of the Gulph where it is narrowest and strongest, until it turns away to go to the southward of the western islands, where it is broader and weaker."

If Franklin expected his suggestion to be accepted as the solution to the problem, a disappointment awaited him. He had not counted on the pride of the packet-boat skippers. Running the finest ships then sailing the ocean, they would brook no suggestions gleaned from the experience of whale fishermen. So they ignored the chart and route Franklin had re-

A CHART of The GULF STREAM

REMARKS

Upon the Navigation from

NEWFOUNDLAND to NEW-YORK,

In order to avoid the

GULPH STREAM

On one hand, and on the other the SHOALS that lie to the Southward of Nantucket and of St. George's Banks.

AFTER you have passed the Banks of Newfoundland in about the 44th degree of latitude, you will meet with nothing, till you draw near the Isle of Sables, which we commonly pass in latitude 43. Southward of the isle, the current is found to extend itself as far North as 41° 20' or 30', then it turns towards the E. S. E. or S. E. ½ E.

Having passed the Isle of Sables, shape your course for the St. George's Banks, so as to pass them in about latitude 40°, because the current southward of those banks reaches as far North as 39°. The shoals of those banks lie in 41° 35'.

After having passed St. George's Banks, you must, to clear Nantucket, form your course so as to pass between the latitudes 38° 30' and 40° 45'.

The most southern part of the current diredly to the south of Nantucket lies in about latitude 38° 30'.

By observing these directions and keeping between the stream and the shoals, the passage from the Bank of Newfoundland to New-York, Delaware, or Virginia, may be considerably shortened; for so you will have the advantage of the eddy current, which moves contrary to the Gulph Stream. Whereas if to avoid the shoals you keep too far to the southward, and get into the stream, you will be retarded by it at the rate of 60 or 70 miles a day.

The Nantucket whale-men being extremely well acquainted with the Gulph Stream, its course, strength and extent, by their constant practice of whaling on the edges of it, from their island quite down to the Bahamas, this draft of that stream was obtained from one of them, Capt. Folger, and caused to be engraved on the old chart in London, for the benefit of navigators, by

B. FRANKLIN.

Note. The Nantucket captains who are acquainted with this stream, make their voyages from England to Boston in as short a time generally as others take in going from Boston to England, viz. from 20 to 30 days.

A stranger may know when he is in the Gulph Stream, by the warmth of the water, which is much greater than that of the water on each side of it. If then he is bound to the westward, he should cross the stream to get out of it as soon as possible.

B. F.

quested from Captain Folger and continued to travel as always over the Gulf Stream. The postal authorities could complain, but they could not command the course of the ships.

Franklin, nevertheless, pursued his study of the Gulf Stream. Whenever he sailed between England and home, he spent many hours testing the temperature of the water, not only by day but sometimes far into the night. On some trips his nephew accompanied him. Then the younger man would take over the task of holding the line attached to the thermometer and weight, letting it out and hauling it up as his uncle directed. The temperature of the Gulf Stream, Franklin discovered, stayed a good bit warmer at all times than the water through which it ran.

Even without taking the temperature, Franklin could always tell when a ship entered the Gulf Stream. Instantly he would notice the thick mass of gulf weed which many years earlier he had tried to analyze. At night, too, the water of the stream looked dull, unlike the rest of the ocean, which sparkled brightly.

During this period Franklin's trips held great danger in a personal sense. In 1776, for example, right after the colonies declared war against England, Franklin set out as a secret agent to France, which, as an enemy of England, might lend its support to the rebels. He left Philadelphia in secrecy, sailing aboard the *Reprisal,* a small American merchant ship converted into a naval vessel. Had a British man-of-war

A CHART OF THE GULF STREAM, TRANSACTIONS OF THE AMERICAN PHILOSOPHICAL SOCIETY, VOL. 2, 1786.

stopped and searched the ship, they would have taken Franklin as a prize prisoner-of-war. In such an event he might have been sent to execution in England. But Franklin hardly had time to worry about this. Day after day, the ship's sails billowing across the Atlantic, he calmly continued his tests and study of the Gulf Stream.

Puzzled as to what made the stream flow through the ocean, he reached this conclusion: Winds from all points of the compass blow across the wide-open expanse of the Atlantic. Some blow for a short time only, caused perhaps by a storm or some other weather condition which changes after a day or two. Others, of a more permanent kind, blow in from a particular direction constantly with little variation in force. To this family belong the trade winds sweeping up from the South Atlantic. And these winds, Franklin believed, help create the Gulf Stream.

Blowing toward the southeastern coast of the colonies, these winds push the ocean water to a higher level in the regions of the Caribbean Sea and the Gulf of Mexico. From these areas the extra, banked-up water flows forth as the Gulf Stream, this warm water passing south of the Florida peninsula and north of the West Indies until it reaches the Atlantic Ocean.

Franklin compared this process to an incident he had seen once while watching a large shallow lake. When a strong wind arose, it blew so hard that it pushed the water to one side of the lake until that part was almost twice as deep as usual, leaving the other half of the lake almost dry. In the same way, you can understand it by watching what happens to a mud puddle after a storm before the wind has died down. Notice how the wind pushes the water to one side of the puddle!

Today we still place great importance on this theory of Franklin's, though scientists believe that opposite flowing ocean currents play a greater part in originating the Gulf Stream. Although Franklin did not discover it, he made the first scientific study of the Gulf Stream. By the time he concluded his research on the subject, he had more information on it than any other person of his time. Through this work, also, he learned a great deal about other maritime and weather conditions. For example, he explained the fogs which hung over the water off the Grand Banks of Newfoundland. As the warm Gulf Stream currents flowed northward, he thought, they met the cooler currents coming down from the Arctic regions near the Newfoundland area. The warm currents, condensed by the cold, made the misty vapors. No one has ever improved on this interpretation to this day.

Franklin's interest in the sea and ships by no means ended here. As in all his experiments, he approached the field like a true scientist, studying his subject thoroughly to the last detail, accepting no idea as fact until he had tested and proved it. Although most of his maritime discoveries had little effect on this branch of science, they remain excellent examples of his amazing persistence in tracking down scientific truth.

CHAPTER NINE

Nautical Inventions and Discoveries

✧✧✧

PERHAPS IF OCEAN travel in his time had offered all the comforts and pleasures it holds now, Franklin would have spent less time on his maritime experiments. Certainly his tests of the Gulf Stream whiled away many tedious hours aboard ship. Boats of that day, run by sail, small in size, offered only cramped living quarters and the barest necessities of furniture: a bed or hammock, a table, and a couple of chairs. Often passengers brought along such food of their own as would keep in order to vary the dull, simple meals served to crew and passengers. Remember, too, that the trip across the ocean took many times as long as it does today.

Before long Franklin started figuring out ways to improve ocean travel: a better design for ships, a new arrangement of sails, safety devices and aids for seamen. Laughed at by shipping authorities, some of his ideas later won acceptance by the industry.

In proposing a new set-up of ship's sails, Franklin pointed out what he believed many seamen overlooked. A ship moves through the air as well as through water. By his design, a number of small sails would replace the single large one. He advised arranging these one behind the other along the cross-trees of the mast. Varying somewhat according to the number of sails used, they would generally cover about the same area as the larger single sail. In this way the ship would carry the same amount of canvas against the wind, but would cut down the resistance to a contrary breeze.

To prove his idea, Franklin performed an experiment with playing cards. Using two cards of equal size, he cut one into eight equal pieces on diagonal lines. These eight parts he strung on two threads, one running through each end of each little card, in such a way that the cards hung exactly above each other evenly spaced in a horizontal line. To the end of each thread he tied a small weight, so that the cards would fall into a straight line. The second playing card he did not cut at all, but simply hung it by theads running through each of its four corners, also weighted down like the smaller cards.

Across the ceiling of the room Franklin now strung a length of twine, fastening to this, about thirty inches apart, two pins bent into the shape of fish hooks. After this he hung on one fish hook the single large card and on the other the set of smaller ones, connect-

ing them by a thread hanging parallel to the twine across the ceiling. Then he cut the string.

If all the cards hit the floor together, it would prove that their resistance to air was equal. But this did not happen. Instead, as Franklin expected, the whole card fell more slowly than the smaller ones, showing that its resistance to air was greater.

Smaller sails, therefore, Franklin believed, would make a ship easier to handle and give it greater speed under adverse winds. The crew could run the sails up or down separately, using more or less sail as required. But he could not convince seamen that the smaller sails would do a better job than the single large one, and they rejected his idea.

Not easily discouraged, he went to work on another project, an improved anchor. While traveling to Europe in a convoy, he noticed that when the breeze rose and the signal came to raise anchor, several of the ships could not do so because their cables, or anchor ropes, parted, leaving their anchors at the bottom of the sea. Franklin asked one of the officers of his ship whether this kind of accident happened often and what caused it. Although the officer did not know the reason, he said it did happen very often.

Before the end of the voyage, Franklin had found a cause and a remedy. Where the cable entered the ship's bow through the hawser hole, he noticed a very sharp bend. As the ship rose or sank with the motion of the sea, the bend strained and slacked at the cable, finally wearing it down until it snapped. Franklin suggested placing a wheel inside the hawser hole and hauling the cable over this. By the use of the wheel, the cable would bend gradually at that point, relieving the strain.

Although this proposal met with the same reception as his multiple sails, Franklin would laugh today if he could know how many modern steamships use the device in one form or another.

For a long time seamen had worried about their problem in getting a storm-tossed ship safely through roaring winds and surging seas. Under storm conditions an ordinary anchor proved worthless because of the depth and violence of the waves. At such times they needed a floating type of anchor, known as a sea-anchor.

On one of his trips to Europe, with the helpful advice of the ship's master, Captain Truxton, Franklin designed such an anchor. First he made a list of the basic features needed in this safety device. He had to make it heavy enough and large enough to hold a ship's head into the wind, helping to keep the ship on its course. Yet the size must allow for easy storing on the ship and easy handling by the seamen, who would have to throw it overboard quickly and fix it properly in the water.

When Franklin completed his model, it looked like an umbrella. The stem had four movable arms, arranged by cleats on the four sides, which could be opened by turning a pin located in the joint, where the arms were joined to the cleats. With its arms open, the anchor formed a cross on which Franklin fastened a square of canvas. To the stem he attached ropes to hold the arms open to a particular distance. At one end of the stem he hung a small bag of ballast, and at the opposite end an empty keg.

FRANKLIN'S SEA ANCHOR

114

Thrown overboard, the anchor would open immediately. Afterward the crew, by using a small rope attached to one end of the anchor, could pull it close to the boat and haul it aboard.

This time Franklin's work received proper recognition. Captain Truxton took the new sea-anchor, improved further by a few alterations, with him on a trip to China. In the Pacific the party met with a severe storm. Quickly the sea-anchor went overboard, helping the ship ride out the tempest safely.

In designing ships in colonial days, seamen often left the interior practically free of any partitions. Now Franklin suggested that, for greater safety, they divide it into many small watertight compartments. By increasing the floating power of the ship, this would reduce the danger of sinking. He had come to this conclusion after hearing many stories of deserted ships which failed to sink though the crew had given up all hope. Franklin suspected that as the water mounted, it loosened empty chests and barrels in the ship's hold, these in turn keeping the vessel afloat.

To start with, Franklin suggested, seamen could keep empty water casks, placing them in strategic spots around the boat to act as lifebuoys in case of a storm. At the same time he pointed out that the Chinese built their ships with the hull divided into small compartments. They had each section tightly caulked so that if a leak started in one place, the water would not flood the whole ship. To Franklin this sounded sensible and wise, but American shippers refused to agree. As an excuse they said it would make for much difficulty in stowing cargo. Finally, however, although many years later, they adopted the Chinese technique.

During the later years of Franklin's life the maritime world stood on the threshold of a great revolution, the substitution of steam for sails. Strangely enough, though Franklin devoted much time and thought to the problem of boat-propulsion, he did not think much of the steamship idea. When James Watt built one of the earliest known models, he came to Franklin for an opinion of the project, only to receive discouragement. For once in his life this great scientific prophet failed to recognize an improvement of the future.

However, other ideas appeared for the use of new power in sailing which impressed Franklin more favorably. In France he saw a method demonstrated, developed by a French scientist, Bernoullie, which worked on water power. Bernoullie fastened an L-shaped tube to the bottom of the inside of the boat. At the top of the stem appeared a funnel-like opening, into which he poured the water. As the water ran downward, it passed into the arm of the L which opened out at the stern under the water. Dipping up the water by the bucketful from the ocean, he poured it into the funnel. Then it rushed out through the stern and moved the boat forward.

Although Franklin liked the method, he no doubt

recognized the extreme crudeness of device. To improve it, he suggested the addition of another L-shaped pipe alongside the first. Near the forward portion of the short arm of the second pipe he attached a pump to suck in water from an opening in the bow of the boat. Then the sucked-up water would flow into the second pipe, running downward and back, thus creating the power.

Pumping water, however, made just as backbreaking a job as dipping it up in buckets. For this reason Franklin suggested the installation of a steam-engine, then called a fire-engine, to do the pumping.

Still better, he thought, instead of using water for power, why not air? Using the same kind of pipes as in Bernoullie's plan, the designer could construct them round or square, about two feet in diameter. Both tubes would contain pistons that moved up or down with the motion of the pump handle. These pistons would contain valves which, with the pistons raised, would open and suck air into the tube. With the pistons lowered, the valves closed and forced the air out. He also suggested the use of valves in the arm, or lower part, of the tubes. As the pump handle went down, the valves closed, forcing the air through the valve extending to the stern and into the water. Pressing against this element, the air would move the craft forward. As the pump handle rose, the valves opened and sucked air in, refilling the tubes and repeating the first action.

In this problem, however, Franklin made a poor choice. Before long the steamboat visualized by Watt came into use, far more practical and efficient than the power methods suggested by Bernoullie or Franklin. Nevertheless, Franklin had left his mark on the science of his beloved sea, as he had done, perhaps more notably, on that of heating, music, medicine, and especially electricity.

CHAPTER TEN

Teacher and Prophet:
"A Hundred Years Hence"

❖❖❖❖❖❖❖❖❖❖❖❖❖❖❖❖❖❖❖❖❖❖❖❖❖❖❖❖❖❖❖❖❖

THROUGHOUT HIS LIFE Franklin made friends with young people. As we have seen, he was a gay, warmhearted person full of humor and fellowship. Such a man always likes children, likes to tell them fairy tales and funny stories, and likes to romp with them.

But Franklin thought of himself as more than just a playmate to boys and girls. He wanted to help them learn and grow in mind as well as in body. Unlike old-fashioned people who frowned, then as now, on the new ideas of the "younger generation," Franklin placed his greatest hopes for a better world in these men and women of the future. Writing to Samuel Johnson in 1750, when he had himself hardly reached middle age, he expressed the belief "that general virtue is more probably to be expected and obtained from the *education* of youth, than from the *exhortation* of adult per-

119

sons; bad habits and vices of the mind being, like diseases of the body, more easily prevented than cured."

When we read Franklin's letters, we find that he corresponded regularly with Mary Stevenson, the young daughter of his English hostess, sending her lively descriptions of some of his simpler experiments and theories. One day in May, 1760, she received a package from Franklin, with a note saying, "I send my good girl the books I mention'd to her last night." What sort of books were these? Were they ordinary story books? As we might expect, they were books about science, "written in the familiar, easy manner, for which the French are so remarkable."

In his letter Franklin gave Mary detailed instructions on how to read these books, instructions which sound almost like those given by parents and teachers today. "I would advise you to read," wrote Franklin, "with a pen in your hand, and enter in a little book short hints of what you find that is curious, or that may be useful; for this will be the best method of imprinting such particulars in your memory." Thus you store up useful skills "for practice on some future occasion" and all sorts of knowledge of the world about you which will serve "at least to adorn and improve your conversation."

In every book we read we find words which we have never seen before. Franklin warned Mary that especially in the ones he enclosed "many of the terms of science are such as you cannot have met with in your common reading and may therefore be unacquainted with." If Mary did not find out the meanings of these unfamiliar words, she could learn very little from her reading. "I think it would be well," Franklin wrote, "for you to have a good dictionary at hand, to consult immediately when you meet with a word you do not comprehend the precise meaning of. This may at first seem troublesome and interrupting; but 'tis a trouble that will daily diminish . . . as you become more acquainted with the terms; and in the mean time you will read with more satisfaction, because with more understanding."

Among the experiments he described to Mary Stevenson, you may remember, was the test he made showing the effect of the heat of the sun on different colors of clothing. In 1761 he wrote her also of an idea he had that might prove valuable to ocean travelers. "If people at sea," he wrote, "distressed by thirst when their fresh water is unfortunately spent, would make bathing-tubs of their empty water-casks, and, filling them with sea water, sit in them an hour or two each day, they might be greatly relieved."

Mary, picturing the passengers dipping up barrels full of salt water, setting them around on deck, and taking turns sitting in them, must have laughed merrily. What a funny game! But Franklin, very much in earnest, gave her several reasons for thinking his theory a sound one. For example, he had often observed "that, however thirsty I may have been before going into the water to swim, I am never long so in the water." So he came to wonder whether a person's body does not possibly have special pores which absorb water, pores "perhaps fine enough in filtering to separate salt from water."

Almost two hundred years later, during World War II, shipwrecked survivors reported how they had quenched their thirst at sea by soaking themselves in water. How glad Franklin would have been to hear these stories and to hear Mary Stevenson say, "You told me so!"

Franklin filled his letters, not only to Mary Stevenson but to all his friends and acquaintances, with vivid stories of hundreds of experiments. Many of them indeed sounded like good games for children. Perhaps this was because Franklin got so much fun out of them himself. Perhaps, too, it was because he looked upon the world with the eyes of a child, never ceasing to marvel at the smallest miracle of nature, proving his theories with the simplest instruments.

Once Franklin and some friends in London opened a bottle of Madeira wine imported from Virginia. As they filled the first glass, out floated three drowned flies. Perhaps the other guests shuddered a little, but not so Franklin. Like a small boy with a spider or a toad, he seized this opportunity to find out whether, as he had heard it said, "drowned flies were capable of being revived by the rays of the sun."

To make the test, he left the flies "exposed to the sun upon a sieve." Then he watched to see what would happen. "In less than three hours two of them began by degrees to recover life. They commenced by some convulsive motions of the thighs, and at length they raised themselves upon their legs, wiped their eyes with their forefeet, beat and brushed their wings with their hind feet, and soon after began to fly." Recalling this incident in a letter to a French friend, Franklin put a chuckle between the lines when he spoke of the flies, which had fallen into the wine at the Virginia bottling company, "finding themselves in Old England without knowing how they came thither." As for the third fly, he "continued lifeless till sunset, when losing all hopes of him, he was thrown away."

In 1783, at the age of seventy-seven, Franklin had not lost his "spirit of inquiry after truth" and his interest in new scientific developments. Living in France, where the first balloon flights in history took place late that summer and all through autumn, he sent reports of the tests to Sir Joseph Banks of England's Royal Society. Was this not his duty "to the Society which does me the honour to reckon me among its members?"

When the first balloon went up, in August, it carried no passengers. High up over the fields it rose and floated along. Finally it started downward again. As it touched the ground, it bounced a little, frightening the audience of superstitious country people. "It is said,"

FIRST BALLOON ASCENSION, 1783, AT ANNONAY, FRANCE

Franklin wrote, that they imagined "there was some living animal in it, and attack'd it with stones and knives, so that it was much mangled."

By November the French scientists had made enough progress to send up a man-carrying balloon. On December 1, Franklin went to watch the second aerial flight of man. About one o'clock in the afternoon

124

the balloon floated off the ground. "All eyes," wrote Franklin, "were gratified with seeing it rise majestically above the buildings, a most beautiful spectacle. When it was about two hundred feet high, the brave adventurers held out and waved a little white pennant, to salute the spectators, who returned loud claps of applause."

This flight covered a longer distance than the earlier ones. From its take-off, the balloon rose to a height which Franklin guessed at as more than twenty-five hundred feet. Then, he wrote, "it appeared to have only horizontal motion." Through a pocket-glass, he told Sir Joseph, he followed its course "till I lost sight first of the men, then of the car, and when I last saw the balloon, it appeared no bigger than a walnut."

After the spectators disbanded, Franklin went home and wrote his report to Banks. However, he did not send it off until the next day, when he could add this postscript: "I am relieved from my anxiety by hearing that the adventurers descended well near L'Isle Adam before sunset . . . near seven leagues from Paris."

The test had been a complete success, the pilots having "perfect command of their carriage, descending as they pleased by letting some of the inflammable air escape, and rising by discharging some sand." Once they swooped "over a field so low as to talk with the labourers in passing, and mounted again to pass a hill." Did Franklin perhaps wish he could have gone along in the balloon to join in this bold sport?

125

But, more than a sport, Franklin saw in these test flights the possibility of "a new turn to human affairs." In January, 1784, he wrote his thoughts on the subject to his old friend Jan Ingenhousz. Who could tell to what use the world might put aerial carriers? What effect might they have on peace and war?

Today we know the answer. Overshadowing its peaceful uses, aviation has made possible greater and more horrible wars than ever before. But Franklin, ever hopeful of knowledge as the road to good rather than evil, suggested to Ingenhousz that this new discovery might succeed in "convincing sovereigns of the folly of wars."

For this conclusion he thought he had a sound basis. "Five thousand balloons, capable of raising two men each, would not cost more than five ships of the line; and where is the prince who can afford so to cover his country with troops for its defence as that ten thousand men descending from the clouds might not in many places do an infinite deal of mischief before a force could be brought together to repel them?"

With this in mind, Franklin eagerly looked forward to the perfection of aerial transportation by scientists of other countries. "It is a pity," he wrote to Ingenhousz, "that any national Jealousy, should, as you may imagine it may, have prevented the English from prosecuting the Experiment, since they are such ingenious Mechanicians, that in their Hands it might have made a more rapid Progress towards Perfection, & all the Utility it is capable of affording."

Now, as Franklin approached the end of his life, he thought about the strides science had made since the time of his boyhood eighty years earlier. He wondered, too, what new discoveries lay in store for generations to come. As he wrote to his friend in 1773, telling the story of the drowned flies, "Having a very ardent desire to see and observe the state of America a hundred years hence, I should prefer to any ordinary death the being immersed in a cask of Madeira wine with a few friends till that time, to be then recalled to life by the solar warmth of my dear country!"

This, Franklin knew, was too great a miracle for the science of his day to perform. Sometimes, perhaps, he thought it just as well. He remembered an incident in his youth, when he was sailing down the Delaware River in a little sloop. The boat had to stand at anchor for some time because the wind had died down. Franklin was restless. "The heat of the sun on the vessel was excessive, the company strangers to me, and not very agreeable." On the bank of the river he saw what looked like a green meadow with a huge tree in its center. Imagining how pleasant it would be to sit in the shade of the tree and read, he asked the captain to put him ashore until the tide turned and they could go on. But when he climbed over the bank, he found the meadow was a marsh, in which he sank to his knees, and swarming with mosquitoes, so that he had to return to the sloop, the laughing-stock of the company.

From that experience he had learned to avoid making "frequent and troublesome changes . . . often for the worse." And so he consoled himself for missing the wonders of the future, remembering all the improvements of his own age, so many of which he himself had provided.

Yet, when he died on April 17, 1790, just three months after his eighty-fourth birthday, he must have uttered a sigh, thinking of his words to Joseph Priestley ten years earlier: "The rapid progress *true* science now makes, occasions my regretting sometimes that I was born too soon." For in a thousand years, he hoped, "Agriculture may diminish its labor and double its produce; all diseases may by sure means be prevented or cured, not excepting even that of old age, and our lives lengthened at pleasure."

5953ᴹ